Realism in Practice

An Appraisal

EDITED BY

DAVIDE ORSI, J. R. AVGUSTIN & MAX NURNUS

E-INTERNATIONAL RELATIONS PUBLISHING

E-International Relations
www.E-IR.info
Bristol, England
2018

ISBN 978-1-910814-37-6 (paperback)
ISBN 978-1-910814-38-3 (e-book)

Production: Michael Tang
Cover Image: DmitryRukhlenko via Depositphotos

A catalogue record for this book is available from the British Library

E-IR Edited Collections

Series Editors: Stephen McGlinchey, Marianna Karakoulaki and Agnieszka Pikulicka-Wilczewska
Copy-editing: Cameran Clayton

Editorial assistance: Jasmine Chorley and Hayden Paulsen

E-IR's Edited Collections are open access scholarly books presented in a format that preferences brevity and accessibility while retaining academic conventions. Each book is available in print and digital versions, and is published under a Creative Commons CC BY-NC 4.0 license. As E-International Relations is committed to open access in the fullest sense, free electronic versions of all of our books, including this one, are available on the E-International Relations website.

Find out more at: http://www.e-ir.info/publications

About the E-International Relations website

E-International Relations (www.E-IR.info) is the world's leading open access website for students and scholars of international politics, reaching over 3 million unique readers. E-IR's daily publications feature expert articles, blogs, reviews and interviews – as well as student learning resources. The website is run by a registered non-profit organisation based in Bristol, England and staffed with an all-volunteer team of students and scholars.

Editors

Davide Orsi (Ph.D. in Politics and International Relations from Cardiff University, 2015) is an Editor-at-Large at E-International Relations. His first book *Michael Oakeshott's Political Philosophy of International Relations: Civil Association and International Society* (Palgrave, 2016) explores the historical and normative dimension of international society by relating Oakeshott's philosophy of civil association to English School theories of international relations. He has published work in journals including the *Journal of International Political Theory, Collingwood and British Idealism Studies,* the *European Legacy,* and the *British Journal for the History of Philosophy.*

J. R. Avgustin (Ph.D. in International Relations from University of Ljubljana, 2016) is an Editor-at-Large at E-International Relations. He is an Associate Tutor at the University of East Anglia, an independent research consultant for Nepal Matters for America and a World Debate Institute Fellow. His main research interests focus on the use of force in international relations, particularly when authorised by the UN Security Council (www. unscramblethesc.org). His publications include articles in *Sociology of Diplomacy: Initial Reading* and *Acta Diplomatica.*

Max Nurnus is a PhD student at the Graduate School of International Studies of Seoul National University and Deputy Articles Editor at E-International Relations.

Acknowledgments

This collected edition would not exist without the support and guidance from Stephen McGlinchey, Editor-in-chief of E-International Relations. We would also like to thank Robert W. Murray for his efforts with bringing clarity of concept to this collection. Most of all, we would like to thank all the contributing authors for their work and their patience.

Davide Orsi, J. R. Avgustin and Max Nurnus

Abstract

The purpose of this collection is to appraise the current relevance and validity of realism as an interpretative tool in contemporary International Relations. All chapters of the book are animated by a theoretical effort to define the conceptual aspects of realism and attempt to establish whether the tradition still provides the necessary conceptual tools to scholars of International Relations. The chapters address important issues in contemporary world politics through the lens of realist theory such as the refugee crisis in Europe and the Middle East; the war against ISIS; the appearance of non-state actors and outlaw agents; the rise of China; cyberwarfare; human rights and humanitarian law. The collection also provides insights on some of the theoretical tenets of classical and structural realism. Overall, the collection shows that, in spite of its many shortcomings, realism still offers an incredibly multifaceted understanding of world politics and enlightens the increasing challenges of world politics.

Contents

Contents

Contributors

Francis A. Beer is Professor Emeritus of Political Science at the University of Colorado. His books include: *Meanings of War and Peace*; *Peace Against War: The Ecology of International Violence* and *Integration and Disintegration in NATO: Processes of Alliance Cohesion and Prospects for Atlantic Community* as well as related monographs on *The Political Economy of Alliances* and *How Much War in History*. He has also co-edited (with Robert Hariman) *Post-Realism: The Rhetorical Turn in International Relations*. His present interests centre on meaning, metaphor and myth in international relations with a particular concern for war and peace.

Koldo Casla earned his PhD at King's College London in July 2017, where he has studied why Western European states promote international human rights norms. His most recent publications are 'The rights we live in: protecting the right to housing in Spain' (IJHR, 20:3, 2016) and 'Dear fellow jurists, human rights are about politics, and that's perfectly fine' (chapter in edited volume Can human rights bring social justice?, 2015).

Anthony J.S. Craig is a PhD candidate in the Department of Politics and International Relations at Cardiff University, and a member of the Research School on Peace and Conflict at the Peace Research Institute Oslo. His PhD research investigates developments in national cyber capabilities across the international system.

Layla Dawood is a Professor at the University of the State of Rio de Janeiro (UERJ). She holds a PhD in International Relations from the Pontifical Catholic University of Rio de Janeiro. She has published papers, book chapters and articles on different issues of the International Security field, including Latin American Security. Her research interests encompass International Relations Theory and International Security with a focus on balancing, nuclear policy and non-proliferation.

Robert Hariman is Professor of Communication Studies at Northwestern University. He is the author of *Political Style: The Artistry of Power* and two volumes co-authored with John Louis Lucaites: *No Caption Needed: Iconic Photographs, Public Culture, and Liberal Democracy*, and *The Public Image: Photography and Civic Spectatorship*. His other publications include edited volumes on popular trials, prudence, post-realism, and the texture of political action. His work has been translated into French and Chinese. Together with John Louis Lucaites he maintains a blog: Nocaptionneeded.com.

Richard Ned Lebow is Professor of International Political Theory in the War Studies Department of King's College London, Bye-Fellow of Pembroke College, University of Cambridge and the James O. Freedman Presidential Professor (Emeritus) of Government at Dartmouth College. His most recent books are *National Identifications and International Relations* (Cambridge 2016), *Avoiding War, Making Peace* (Palgrave 2017), and *Max Weber and International Relations* (Cambridge 2017).

Tony Chih-Chi Lee is postdoctoral researcher at the Institute of Asia and African Studies of Humboldt Universität zu Berlin where he pursues a habilitation (German certificat for professorship). His research interests range from area studies (China, in particular) to political psychology. He is particularly keen on deciphering psychological incentives behind decision makings of political leaders or/and leadership groups. His most recent article *Cold Case: Re-investigate the group dynamics of the Chinese Leadership in the 1989 Tiananmen Incident* will be published by the American Journal of Chinese Studies.

Stephen McGlinchey is Senior Lecturer of International Relations at the University of the West of England, Bristol. His most recent books are *International Relations* (E-International Relations 2017) and *US Arms Policies Towards the Shah's Iran* (Routledge 2014). He is the Editor-in-Chief of E-International Relations (www.E-IR.info).

Robert W. Murray is Managing Director of the Government Affairs and Public Policy Practice Group at Dentons Canada LLP and a Research Fellow at the University of Calgary's Centre for Military, Security and Strategic Studies. His recent publications include *Protecting Human Rights in the 21st Century* with Aidan Hehir (Routledge 2017), *Seeking Order in Anarchy: Multilateralism as State Strategy* (University of Alberta Press 2016), and *System, Society and the World: Exploring the English School of International Relations* 2nd Edition (E-International Relations 2015).

Arash Heydarian Pashakhanlou is Assistant Professor in War Studies at the Swedish Defence University. He has published extensively on realism and his latest monograph *Realism and Fear in International Relations: Morgenthau, Waltz and Mearsheimer Reconsidered* was published by Palgrave.

M.J. Peterson is a Professor of Political Science at the University of Massachusetts Amherst (USA). Her research focuses on formal organisations and informal practices through which governments pursue cooperative efforts to address cross-border problems. She is the author of *International Regimes for the Final Frontier* (2005), *Managing the Frozen South: The Creation and*

Evolution of the Antarctic Treaty Regime (1988) and *The General Assembly in World Policies* (1986). She has also authored articles in the *American Political Science Review, the American Journal of International Law, International Organization* and *Review of International Organizations*.

Carsten Rauch is Research Fellow at the Peace Research Institute Frankfurt (PRIF). He received his PhD from Goethe University, Frankfurt in 2013. His research has dealt with the rise and fall of great powers, revisionism in the international system, power transition theory and more generally IR theory, as well as Indian foreign policy. His book publications include *Die Theorie des Demokratischen Friedens* (Campus, 2005), and *Das Konzept des friedlichen Machtübergangs* (Nomos, 2014). He has also published articles in *Security Studies, International Area Studies Review, European Review of International Studies* and *Zeitschrift für Friedens- und Konfliktforschung*.

Felix Rösch is Senior Lecturer in International Relations at Coventry University. He works on encounters of difference in transcultural and intercultural contexts at the intersection of classical realism and critical theories. He has published articles in *Review of International Studies, European Journal of International Relations, International Studies Perspectives* and *Ethics & International Affairs*. His most recent books include *The Concept of the Political* (2012), *Émigré Scholars and the Genesis of International Relations* (2014), and *Power, Knowledge, and Dissent in Morgenthau's Worldview* (2015).

Archie W. Simpson is a teaching fellow in Politics and International Relations at the University of Bath. He has previously taught at the University of Aberdeen, University of St Andrews, University of Stirling and University of Nottingham. He is a founding member of the Centre for Small State Studies at the University of Iceland and is on the international editorial board of the new journal *Small States and Territories*. His main research interests are in small states, international security, grand strategy and European politics.

Brandon Valeriano is the Donald Bren Chair of Armed Politics at the Marine Corps University and a Reader in the Department of Politics and International Relations at Cardiff University. He also serves as an adjunct fellow for the Niskanen Center. His two most recent books are *Cyber War versus Cyber Reality* at Oxford University Press (2015) and *Russia's Coercive Diplomacy* at Palgrave (2015).

Anders Wivel is a Professor of Political Science at the University of Copenhagen. His research interests include political realism, power politics and foreign policy, in particular the foreign policy of small states. His articles have appeared in various journals including *Cooperation and Conflict, Journal of Common Market Studies, Security Dialogue, Cambridge Review of International Affairs, Journal of International Relations and Development* and *European Security.* His most recent book is *The Routledge Handbook of Scandinavian Politics* (Routledge, 2017) (co-edited with Peter Nedergaard).

Introduction

The Practice of Realism in International Relations

DAVIDE ORSI, J. R. AVGUSTIN AND MAX NURNUS

Realism in International Relations can be considered as the discipline's oldest theory, having its first advocate in Thucydides, who presented the idea that power trumps justice and morality in *The Peloponnesian War*. Among many others, Machiavelli and Hobbes, first, E.H. Carr and H. Morgenthau, then, offered to their readers provocative and eternal questions that still challenge our times (Boucher 1998, 47–170; Molloy 2006). In a way, realism (also with its more contemporary versions with Waltz and Mearsheimer) can be considered as one of the most enduring approaches in IR. One of the reasons for this is that 'it sets itself up as a no-nonsense practical science of international politics' (Sutch and Elias 2007, 42). In realism, all events in international politics make sense and can be explained through relatively clear and immediate principles. For these reasons, realism not only remains a cornerstone of International Relations theory (Gold and McGlinchey 2017, 46–49), but also a thriving approach in the broad fields of political studies and political theory (Bell 2017). Classical realism has shaped the way in which the relations between states over the centuries have been understood and still influences policymakers today. According to some observers, realism has determined the foreign policies of both Barack Obama (Pillar 2016) and Donald Trump (Cole 2017).

On the other hand, realism is often challenged by the changing circumstances of contemporary world politics. For example, the notion of timeless principles and human nature, which are 'unaffected by the circumstances of time and place' (Morgenthau 1985, 10–11), has often been considered as an abstraction, more useful to understand realism as a theory than world politics. Among many other possible issues with realism, recent events such as the rise of non-state actors and non-conventional confrontation between international agents made the often state-centric realist view more and more fragile. Already in a 1995 article, Ethan Kapstein argued that realism in

International Relations might be 'deeply and perhaps fatally flawed' yet 'continues to define the discipline' (1995, 751). Not long after, Jeffrey Legro and Andrew Moravcsik also saw a dominant role of Realist voices, while at the same time perceiving realism 'in trouble' and 'in need of reformulation' (1999, 5, 54). Today, realism is again accused of being grounded on 'astonishingly bold' claims and 'empirically unprovable' tenets (Motyl 2015) and of being unable to explain the complex reality of world politics.

The purpose of this collection is not to solve this dilemma; it is not to establish whether realism should be considered as the bearer of eternal truths regarding world politics or whether it should be abandoned. This book takes instead a more limited and nuanced approach, by appraising the current relevance and validity of realism as an interpretative tool in contemporary International Relations. In this spirit, all chapters of the book are animated not only by a theoretical effort to define the conceptual aspects of realism, but also by the aim of finding whether the tradition still provides the necessary conceptual tools to practitioners and scholars of International Relations.

In the chapter that opens the volume Lebow and Rösch present some of the perennial ideas that have shaped the realist tradition in international thought. By challenging the common reading that sees profound differences among various schools of realism (structural, classical, neo-positivist, and more), Lebow and Rösch find some essential elements of realism. These are the 'tragic vision of life' and the controversial relation between ethics and power. However, Lebow and Rösch not only offer this important interpretation but also claim that, on this ground, realism can still enlighten our understanding of world politics, by offering critical insights on the refugee crisis in Europe and the Middle East.

In the second chapter, Beer and Hariman show the persistent relevance of realist thinking in International Relations with regard to the rise of ISIS. To this end, they take a different approach from that of Lebow and Rösch and present an updated version of realism: post-realism, which seeks to offer a much more accurate account of the immaterial and cultural aspects of international politics.

Several contributions try to assess whether realism still offers a valuable instrument for the understanding of the world after the end of the Cold War. Pashakhanlou (Chapter 3) evaluates the explanatory power of Waltz's defensive realism and Mearsheimer's offensive realism in the light of the challenges of the allegedly unipolar post-Cold War world. In this light, a series of chapters addresses the rise of China in the post-Cold War era. Lee (Chapter 4) identifies the main challenge to realism in the rise of China's soft power and in the theoretical shortcomings of the conception of power as it is defined by various realist schools. Chapter 5 by Carsten Rauch examines the case of China by comparing the realist approach to Power Transition Theory. Dawood (Chapter 6) analytically examines the Chinese balancing role towards the USA, with particular regard to the problem of the South-China Sea and the building up of China's naval power.

War has always been at the centre of realist theory. The activities of hackers during elections and the disruptions they caused against public services and governments (for example the attack against the NHS in Britain in May 2017) show the growing importance of this new important level of confrontation among states, which is examined in the contribution (Chapter 7) by Craig and Valeriano on cybersecurity.

In Chapter 8 Anders Wivel focuses on 'peaceful change' as an instrument of international politics in its relation to power. Despite being recognised by E.H. Carr as one of the fundamental problems in international morality and law (see below), realist thinking has rarely considered the problem. In Chapter 9, Simpson examines the issue of small states and neutrality, challenging the traditional realist interest in great powers. By offering an historical excursus from the Melian dialogue to the post-Cold War era, the author examines the place of neutrality in contemporary politics, shaped by the return of multipolar politics.

One of the characters of realist theory is to identify a tension between ideals, and normative frameworks, and political reality. In contemporary politics, the *lingua franca* that shapes our normative expectations towards political actors is set by human rights. McGlinchey and Murray examine the American policy in the Middle-East during the Carter presidency and show the continuous tension between systemic pressure and ideals, including human rights and disarmament (Chapter 10). On a more theoretical level, and in the light of the growing literature of the politics of international law, Casla challenges this traditional view and finds instead that traditional realism offers substantial arguments for the relevance of International Human Rights Law in world politics (Chapter 11). The conclusive contribution (Chapter 12) by Peterson identifies in the persistence of power politics the main reason of the continuing relevance of realism in international relations.

All the chapters included in this volume rise from an urgent practical need: that of understanding the changing landscape of contemporary international politics. The relative decline of American power, the ambivalent Russian return and the rise of China, as well as the threats posed by non-state actors and new forms of military might are the problem felt by scholars in international politics as well as by the educated public. Notwithstanding the many critiques that the chapters of this volume advance against classical realist thinkers, what emerges is that realism offers an incredibly multifaceted understanding of world politics and enlightens the increasing challenges of world politics.

References

Bell, Duncan. ed. 2008. *Political Thought and International Relations. Variations on a Realist Theme.* Oxford: Oxford University Press.

Bell, Duncan. 2017. "Political Realism and International Relations." *Philosophy Compass* 12(2): 1–12.

Boucher, David. 1998. *Political Theories of International Relations.* Oxford: Oxford University Press.

Cole, Phil. 2017. "Trumpism and the Future of International Politics: The Return of Realism." *E-International Relations* (http://www.e-ir.info/2017/01/29/trumpism-and-the-future-of-international-politics/) accessed 25/06/2017.

Gold, Dana and Stephen McGlinchey. 2017. "International Relations Theory." *International Relations.* Edited by Stephen McGlinchey, 46–56. Bristol: E-International Relations.

Kapstein, Ethan B. 1995. "Is Realism Dead? The Domestic Source of International Politics." *International Organization* 49 (4): 751–774.

Legro, Jeffrey W and Andrew Moravcsik. 1999. "Is Anybody Still a Realist?" *International Security* 24(2): 5–55.

Molloy, Sean. 2006. *The Hidden History of Realism. A Genealogy of Power Politics.* London: Palgrave.

Morgenthau, Hans. 1985. *Politics among Nations. The Pursuit of Power and Peace.* Chicago, IL: Chicago University Press.

Motyl, Alexander J. 2015. "The Surrealism of Realism: Misreading the War in Ukraine." *World Affairs* (http://www.worldaffairsjournal.org/article/surrealism-realism-misreading-war-ukraine, accessed on 25/06/2017).

Pillar, Paul. 2016. "Obama the Realist." *National Interest* (http://nationalinterest.org/blog/paul-pillar/obama-the-realist-15479?page=show, accessed 25/06/2017).

Sutch, Peter and Juanita Elias. 2007. *International Relations: The Basics*. London: Routledge.

1

Realism: Tragedy, Power and the Refugee Crisis

FELIX RÖSCH & RICHARD NED LEBOW

Since the end of the Cold War realism has returned to its roots. Realist scholars show renewed interest in their paradigm's foundational thinkers, their tragic understanding of life and politics, their practical concern for ethics, and their understanding of theory as the starting point for explanatory narratives or forward-looking forecasts that are highly context dependent. In this chapter, we do not attempt to map these recent re-readings. Despite their different perspectives on world politics, the writings of Thucydides, Niccolò Machiavelli, E. H. Carr, Reinhold Niebuhr, Arnold Wolfers, John Herz, Hans Morgenthau, and Hannah Arendt demonstrate a remarkable unity of thought, as they have been driven by similar concerns about 'perennial problems' (Morgenthau 1962, 19). One of these problems is the depoliticisation of societies. Realists were concerned that, in modern societies, people could no longer freely express their interests in public, losing the ability to collectively contribute to their societies. Consequently, realism can be perceived as a critique of and 'corrective' (Cozette 2008, 12) to this development.

To introduce this perspective of realism and to understand the differences between neorealism and realism (also Bell 2017), we particularly focus on mid-twentieth century realists which are often now identified as classical realists in the literature. This micro-lens on realism is possible because, due to their common war and even migration experiences, their thoughts resonate with each other particularly well. In the first section, we outline realism's tragic understanding of life and how to deal with it. This is followed in the second section by an introduction into one of the core realist concepts – power – before arguing that realism does not promote a world of nation-states. Finally, we discuss the current refugee crisis through a realist perspective.

The Tragic Vision of Life

Mid-twentieth century realists were a diverse group of scholars. Although their geographical centre was in the United States, with exceptions like Carr and Georg Schwarzenberger in the United Kingdom and Raymond Aron in France, many of them were émigrés from Europe, who had been forced to leave due to the rise of fascism and communism. Although they shared a common humanistic worldview in the sense that they had received similar extensive secondary schooling in liberal arts and they believed that people can only experience themselves as human beings by engaging with others in the public sphere, their diversity is also evidenced in their wide range of professions. Given that IR was only gradually institutionalised in Europe when the first chair was set up in light of the horrors of World War I at the university in Aberystwyth, Wales in 1919, none of them was trained as an IR scholar. Instead, they were historians, sociologists, philosophers, lawyers, and even theologians. Only retrospectively were many of them linked to IR. Even Morgenthau, arguably the most well-known realist, held a professorship for political science and history – not for international politics. Despite this diversity, however, mid-twentieth century realists agreed on a tragic vision of life; a view they shared with many of their predecessors (Lebow 2003; Williams 2005). This is because people, and more so leaders, have to make decisions on the basis of incomplete information, deal with unpredictability of their actions, and cope with irreconcilable value conflicts within and among societies. Above all, they recognise that leaders must sometimes resort to unethical means (e.g. violence) to achieve laudable ends, and without prior knowledge that these means will accomplish the ends they seek.

This tragic outlook is understandable if we consider the contexts in which classical realists wrote. Thucydides lived during the times of the Peloponnesian War in which Athens lost its pre-eminence in the ancient Greek world. Machiavelli's life was also influenced by repetitive conflicts in which papal, French, Spanish, and other forces aimed to seize control over Northern Italy during the Renaissance Wars (1494–1559). Modern realists finally experienced with the rise of ideologies the climax of a development that had started almost 200 years earlier. Since the Age of Enlightenment culminating in the French Revolution, people were freed from religious straightjackets, but at the same time had lost a sense of community that ideologies like nationalism, liberalism, or Marxism could only superficially restore, and often only at the cost of violent conflicts. Realists shared public sentiments that losing this sense of community caused a decline of commonly accepted values as exemplified in the German debate on a cultural crisis during the early decades of the twentieth century and it made them more susceptible to the temptations of ideologies. This is because ideologies provide what Arendt (1952, 469) called 'world explanations', enabling people to channel their human drives into them.

John Herz (1951) argued that the drive for self-preservation, which ensures that people care about their survival in the world by seeking food and shelter, provokes a security dilemma because people can never be certain to avoid attacks from others. Morgenthau (1930), by contrast, was more concerned about people's drive to prove themselves, achieved by making contributions to their social-political life worlds. Success is difficult because people have incomplete knowledge about themselves and their life-worlds. Any political decision must always be temporary and subject to revision if circumstances change or knowledge is being advanced. In realising that their ambitions are in vain, another tragic aspect of life comes to the fore. For Morgenthau, accepting this tragic aspect is a first step toward transcending it; people can reflect critically about their existence and come to understand that only through their own efforts can life become meaningful.

In modernity, however, having lost values as a basis to make informed judgements, peoples' lives are characterised by what Stephen Toulmin (1990, 35) called a 'quest for certainty', but only few manage to deal with the hardships self-critical contemplation entails. Most, as Nietzsche noted, content themselves with the illusions of being embedded in some form of community. As Morgenthau (n.d., 2) put it: 'being imperfect and striving toward perfection, man ought not to be alone. For while the companionship of others cannot make him perfect, it can supplement his imperfection and give him the illusion of being perfect.' Therefore, also on the level of nation-states tragedy looms large because both drives urge people to live in political communities which are characterised by the same deficiencies that hamper the human condition.

Power and Ethics

Given that these drives affect people on every level, realists do not distinguish between domestic and international politics. Rather, they focus on political communities however they may be conceived because it is through peoples' relations that these human drives start to affect politics.

In these relations, power plays a decisive role. Due to the drive to prove oneself, a balance of power evolves in interpersonal, intergroup, and international relations to counter the development of hegemonic power (Morgenthau 1948). This balance of power is not stable but evolving because actors face a security dilemma (Herz 1951). Due to uncertainty, actors live in fear and they are constantly striving to amass further power only causing the same reaction in their potential adversaries. Hence, it is less physical or material constraints that lead to a balance of power, but it is the result of emotional insecurity. Ironically, therefore, balance of power works best when needed least because if people and communities share some form of common identity, they can cooperate more easily and would not require a balance of power.

Human drives however have an even more dramatic effect on societies beyond the evolvement of a balance of power, as they can depoliticise them. This concern is central to the realist thought of Herz, Arendt, or Niebuhr. Particularly insightful in this respect is Morgenthau (Rösch 2014, 2015). With his understanding of the political, he opposed the more common friend-enemy distinction by the German jurist Carl Schmitt. Morgenthau (2012) defined the political as a universal force that is inherent in every human and that necessarily focuses on others, while at the same time it only comes into being in interpersonal relationships. The resulting discussions, in which people express their interests, create an 'arena of contestation' (Galston 2010, 391). Realising their individual capabilities and experiencing power through acting together, people develop their identities, as they gain knowledge about themselves and their life-worlds. The tragedy of human imperfection, however, endangers the political, as it fosters the development of ideologies. Given that most people cannot face their imperfections, ideologies offer some form of ontological security. This means that ideologies provide people with a sense of order and help them to conceal the initial meaninglessness of life by offering explanations to historical and current socio-political events. Particularly fascism and communism occupied realist thought as they were the most violent ideologies during the lifetime of mid-twentieth century realists, but they were also critical of the hubris of American liberalism and nationalism in general.

For realists, ideologies aim to retain the socio-political *status quo* and any human activity has to be geared towards sustaining this reification. The current socio-political reality is being perceived as given and it cannot be fundamentally altered. The development of the political as an 'arena of contestation', however, endangers this socio-political *status quo*, as it enables people to voice their interests and share their thoughts about the composition and purpose of their political community, eventually opening up the potential of socio-political change. To cope with this depoliticisation, realists advertised what can be called an 'ethics of responsibility' – to use Max Weber's term. Although realists were convinced that most people would be unwilling or incapable of taking responsibility for their lives, they still argued for an ethics in which decision-making is guided by 'intellectual honesty' (Sigwart 2013, 429). Thoughts and beliefs have to be contextualised in a self-critical process that demonstrates empathy towards the position of others. The resulting 'discourse ethic', as Arendt called it, can only happen in collectivity and

American town hall meetings provided the perfecting setting for Arendt, as they allow all people who share a common interest to congregate. As a consequence, however, people have to be prepared to change their positions and be willing to take responsibility for the moral dilemmas of (inter)national politics.

The Nation-State and the Possibility of a World State

Contrary to common assumptions, realists are not apologists of the nation-state, but critical of it, aiming to avoid its dangers and transcend its shortcomings by investigating the potential of a world state (Scheuerman 2011).

For a variety of reasons, classical realists considered nation-states to be 'blind and potent monster[s]' (Morgenthau 1962, 61). They are blind because globalisation and technological advancements not only hinder them to fulfill their role of providing security, but they endanger life on earth altogether. Particularly strong versions of this critique can be found in Aron, Herz, and Morgenthau. The latter provided a disenchanted view on the prospects of humanity in one of his last public appearances, arguing that 'we are living in a dream world' (Morgenthau 1979, 42) because nation-states can no longer uphold the claim to have a monopoly of power over a given territory with the development of nuclear weapons. Furthermore, the squandering of natural resources threatens the environment, leading to a 'society of waste' (Morgenthau 1972, 23). However, nation-states are also potent because in gaining sovereignty over a specific territory and a specific group of people, they exert violence on these people and on others. Nation-states universalise their own standards and even try to impose them onto others, as evidenced in the rise of fascism during the early twentieth century in Europe. After seizing power in countries like Italy, Germany, Spain, and Croatia, fascist movements not only waged wars internationally as exemplified in Germany's invasion in Poland, leading to World War II, and Italy's Abyssinian War (1935–1936) with the intention to gain control over Ethiopia, but they also exerted violence domestically by ostracising ethnic, religious, and socio-political minorities. Furthermore, technological advancements complicate human life-worlds, accelerating socio-political decision-making processes. This benefited the development of scientific elites, who are unaccountable to the public, but who in their attempt to socially plan the world affect people in their everyday lives greatly.

Given that classical realists were sceptical of the promises of modern nation-states, they argued for the establishment of a world community, eventually leading to a world state. Such a global community can help to transcend the depoliticisation in modern societies and even support 'defenders of the global state to stay sober' (Scheuerman 2011, 150). By enabling people to get together on various different levels, political spheres can extrapolate beyond national borders, allowing people to exchange their interests globally and gradually develop an identity that goes beyond that of the nation-state. Their flexibility allows people to accommodate diverse human interests. The resulting self-reflexivity and open-mindedness helps to accept different life trajectories which are influenced by historical, cultural, socio-political or religious factors. In political spheres, people are acknowledged for their differences and, through discussions, a common ground is established that suits everybody. Realists did not arrive at this conclusion straight away. Rather, scholars like Morgenthau and Niebuhr were sceptical at first of the United Nations and the precursors of the European Union, but they realised that they provide the space for the political to gradually evolve, as different actors can get together peacefully and exchange their ideas.

Realist Epistemologies and the Refugee Crisis in Europe and the Middle East

To demonstrate the potential of realism for twenty-first century IR-theorising, we refer to the current refugee crisis in Europe and the Middle East. In 2016, more than 4.5 million people were displaced from Syria, of which an estimated 2.5 million were living in Turkey at that time and more than 800,000 applications for asylum have reached the EU (European Commission 2016). Focusing on this crisis might not seem to be an obvious choice, but many realists, who made their career in the United States, were refugees themselves (Lebow 2011). Indeed, Herz (1984, 9) characterised himself as a 'traveller between all worlds' and Morgenthau even was a 'double exile' (Frankfurter 1937) after his expulsion from Germany and later Spain before arriving in the United States in 1937. Our aim is to demonstrate that realism provides useful insights into this crisis, as we can investigate the conditions for a peaceful coexistence of differences. This is important, as refugees have been identified as one of the reasons why the British public has voted to leave the EU in 2016 and the rise of right-wing parties throughout Europe further suggests that refugees are being pictured in security discourses as a threat.

Relating the work of mid-twentieth century realists to this development enables IR-scholarship to understand that security is established in a discursive context, making it dependent on spatial-temporal conditions. This means security has different meanings in different contexts and therefore it is transformative (Behr 2013, 169). This aspect rests on the insights that realists gained through the study of Karl Mannheim's (1985) *Ideology and Utopia* which was first published in 1929. One of the key concepts that we find in this book is the conditionality of knowledge which means that knowledge is always bound to the socio-political environment in which it operates, stressing that universal knowledge is impossible. Applying this notion on the current refugee crisis, we understand that perceiving refugees as a threat to security is the result of human will and political agency. For example, the refugee crisis was one of the dominant drivers of British Brexit-discourses, although the UK received less than 40,000 asylum seekers in 2015. By comparison, more than 400,000 refugees chose Germany as their destination and Sweden received more than 160,000 in the same period, making the latter the European country that has accepted most refugees in relation to the overall population (British Red Cross 2016).

This is not to say that this process always takes place consciously, as we can never be entirely sure how our writings or actions are perceived by others, but classical realism can help us to understand that humans are not only the objects of security, but also its subjects. In public discourses, they have to have the possibility to redefine the substance of security, instead of leaving it to (inter)national foreign policy elites. As mentioned, these discourses have to include all involved people, and given that different interests morph into a common good, they evolve antagonistically without causing violent outbreaks, if, following Morgenthau, all interests are taken into account. To make this process work, however, dialogical learning is required, as contemporary scholarship calls it. This form of learning is based on continuous possibilities of exchange between refugees and local people and it requires refugees and locals to demonstrate open-mindedness and empathy as well as the willingness to challenge one's own positions. As a result, security can be redefined and what is perceived to be a crisis can be eventually understood as an opportunity to create something 'which did not exist before, which was not given, not even as an object of cognition or imagination' (Arendt 1961, 151).

Conclusion

In this chapter, we have introduced a reading of realism that is probably uncommon. Realism is often confused with neorealism, making students believe that realism provides explanations for the current international political status quo. By contrast, it was our ambition to offer a more nuanced picture of realism and to demonstrate that realism helps in developing a more critical awareness of international politics. To demonstrate this potential, the refugee crisis in Europe and the Middle East was chosen as a case study. Realism does not provide a one-stop solution to this crisis, but it acts as a critical corrective to political discourses that securitise refugees in the sense that they are made into a question of security which in turn justifies the use of extraordinary means to police this threat. Rather, realism encourages to transform the differences that are perceived as a security issue into a potential to create more inclusive societies. Realism is therefore far from being a case for the dustbin of the history of international political thought, as some commentators on realism suggest, but it can serve as a stepping stone to question some of the common assumptions held in the discipline.

References

Arendt, Hannah. 1961. *Between Past and Future. Six Exercises in Political Thought*. London: Faber & Faber.

Arendt, Hannah. 1952. *The Origins of Totalitarianism.* Cleveland: World Publishing.

Behr, Hartmut. 2013. "Security Politics and Public Discourse: A Morgenthauian Approach", *Interpreting Global Security*, edited by Mark Bevir, Oliver Daddow, and Ian Hall. London: Routledge, 160–176.

Bell, Duncan. 2017. "Political Realism and International Relations", *Philosophy Compass* 12(2): 1–12.

British Red Cross. 2016. "Refugee Facts and Figures". (http://ow.ly/ZG3d6, Accessed 18 March 2016)

Cozette, Murielle. 2008. "Reclaiming the Critical Dimension of Realism: Hans J. Morgenthau and the Ethics of Scholarship", *Review of International Studies* 34(1): 5–27.

European Commission. 2016. "Syria Crisis. Echo Factsheet". (http://ow.ly/ZG34q, Accessed 18 March 2016).

Frankfurter, Felix. 1937. Letter to Nathan Greene, 9 December (Container 22, Manuscript Division, Library of Congress, Washington, DC).

Galston, William A. 2010. "Realism in Political Theory", *European Journal of Political Theory* 9(4): 385–411.

Herz, John. 1951. *Political Realism and Political Idealism*. Chicago: University of Chicago Press.

Herz, John. 1984. *Vom Überleben. Wie ein Weltbild entstand*. Düsseldorf: Droste.

Lebow, Richard N. 2003. *The Tragic Vision of Politics. Ethics, Interests, and Orders*. Cambridge: Cambridge University Press.

Lebow, Richard N. 2011. "German Jews and American Realism", *Constellations* 18(4): 545–566.

Mannheim, Karl. 1985. *Ideology & Utopia. An Introduction to the Sociology of Knowledge*. San Diego: Harcourt.

Morgenthau, Hans J. (n.d.) *The Significance of Being Alone* (Container 4, Folder 6, Hans Morgenthau Collection, Leo Baeck Institute Archives, New York).

Morgenthau, Hans J. 1930. *Über die Herkunft des Politischen aus dem Wesen des Menschen* (Container 151, Manuscript Division, Library of Congress, Washington, D.C.).

Morgenthau, Hans J. 1948. "The twilight of international morality", *Ethics* 58(2): 79–99.

Morgenthau, Hans J. 1962. *Politics in the Twentieth Century. Volume I. The Decline of Democratic Politics*. Chicago: University of Chicago Press.

Morgenthau, Hans J. 1972. *Science: Servant or Master?* New York: New American Library.

Morgenthau, Hans J. 1979. *Human Rights and Foreign Policy*. New York: Council on Religion and International Affairs.

Morgenthau, Hans J. 2012. *The Concept of the Political*, edited by Hartmut Behr and Felix Rösch. Basingstoke: Palgrave Macmillan.

Rösch, Felix. 2014. "Pouvoir, Puissance, and Politics: Hans Morgenthau's Dualistic Concept of Power?", *Review of International Studies* 40(2): 349–365.

Rösch, Felix. 2015. *Power, Knowledge, and Dissent in Morgenthau's Worldview*. New York: Palgrave Macmillan.

Scheuerman, William E. 2011. *The Realist Case for Global Reform* Cambridge: Polity Press.

Sigwart, Hans-Jörg. 2013. "The Logic of Legitimacy: Ethics in Political Realism", *Review of Politics* 75(3): 407–432.

Toulmin, Stephen. 1990. *Cosmopolis. The Hidden Agenda of Modernity.* Chicago: University of Chicago Press.

Williams, Michael E. 2005. *The Realist Tradition and the Limits of International Relations*. Cambridge: Cambridge University Press.

2

Realism, Post-Realism and ISIS

FRANCIS A. BEER & ROBERT HARIMAN

International realism has many branches. Beginning with historical thinkers such as Thucydides, Machiavelli, and Hobbes, the realist narrative has swept forward through time to practitioners such as Richelieu, Bismarck, and Kissinger, and writers such as Morgenthau, Waltz, and Mearsheimer. Analysts of realism have grouped contemporary realists into different schools. These include classical realism, traditional realism, neo-realism, neo-classical realism, structural realism, liberal realism, left realism, offensive realism, defensive realism and others (see e.g. Bew 2015; Elman and Jensen 2014). The potential list of realisms seems limited only by the finitude of adjectives.

At the risk of contributing to further theoretical overpopulation, we here present another variant: post-realism. Post-realism begins by anchoring itself in the tenets of traditional realism, and then adjusting them. It adapts historical realism to a contemporary evolutionary path, appropriate for complex globalising society. According to a standard realist narrative, states are the major actors in international relations. They are motivated mainly by interests in maximising power. They extend their domestic monopolies of violence onto anarchical international society through military actions and war. Post-realism does not reject these elements but incorporates them into a larger, more intricate story. Yes, states are substantial, but there are other significant actors. Yes, interests and power matter, but there are other motivations. Yes, military actions and war are important, but there are other noteworthy forms of global action. (cf. Legro and Moravcsik 1999; Beer and Hariman 1996, 2004). In any event, the essential realist narrative, as we understand it, hardly reflects, or even guides, the actual practice of most international relations scholars or the mechanics of actual day-to-day governmental and non-governmental foreign policy operations — political, military, economic, social, cultural, or technological. Here, professionals operate within their own regimes and disciplines, epistemic communities and knowledge-based networks, private languages and political bases. They have their own motivations and worlds of meaning, exercising important policy influence very far from the direct guidance of realist theory (cf. Cross 2013; Haas 1991).

Instead of a reduction to a few variables of states — interests, capability to project power, credibility, and the like — post-realism directs attention to those points where individual actors or the system as a whole may appear less comprehensible or consistent through a traditional realist lens. Post-realism aims to refocus realism with a higher fidelity real-time picture: thicker description, more intricate explanation, more nuanced prediction, and a better toolbox for policy-makers trying to understand and navigate the multifaceted modern world in which we live. Below, we illustrate post-realism's utility using the example of ISIS.

More than States

Post-realism, like realism, begins with states as actors. At the same time, it goes beyond states to include a wide variety of non-state actors within the mix of players on the world stage. These comprise various networks of governmental and non-governmental actors combined in supra-national, national, sub-national forms.

One set of such actors include militant groups such as Al Qaeda, Boko Haram, Hamas, Hezbollah, Shabab, the Taliban — and ISIS, the Islamic State of Iraq and Syria, also known by other names including Daesh or ISIL (see Gerges 2016; Nance 2016, 20). We focus specifically on this last group, to which we shall refer as ISIS, which is a multidimensional, quasi-state/national actor. It has its own global, regional, and local networks with links to other networks. It emphasises specific issues; it combines acts of violence against enemies with social services to its clients. It has created a distinctive presence in global media and discussions of foreign policy.

ISIS aspires to be a state; the Islamic State in Syria, Iraq, the Levant, and elsewhere. But it has much larger ambitions. The Caliphate, if successful, would eventually expand to the *ummah*, the entire community of the Islamic faithful. It harkens back to the past as it points toward the future; it is thus pre-national and post-national, pre-colonial and post-colonial, pre-realist and post-realist. In this quest, ISIS aims at continuing the deconstruction and reconstruction of the remains of the old empires. The most immediate target includes the vestiges of the former Ottoman Sultanate. But ISIS also aims to demolish the remains of the Sykes–Picot Agreement of 1916 between Britain and France, with the consent of Russia. This agreement, together with the Balfour Declaration of 1917, from the United Kingdom's Foreign Secretary

Arthur James Balfour to Baron Rothschild, helped establish the political framework ordering the Middle East. Ironically, the successors to the old imperial European states have themselves engaged in their own post-realist rebellion against the Westphalian state system. They have simultaneously hoped to subsume themselves into a larger European supra-national community, and to make all borders more porous for flows of capital, labour, and information. Tribal, national, and post-national domains are thus parallel worlds for ISIS and other actors where post-realism is an emerging common sense.

More than Interest and Power

Post-realism, like realism, suggests that political actors are driven, if they are to survive, by national self-interest defined primarily by considerations of power. Post-realism, however, goes beyond self-interest and power to include many other motivations, goals, and intentions implicit in economics, society, and culture as well as multiple other frames — metaphors and narratives; ideas, ideologies, and identities; mentalities and cognitions; emotions and attitudes — that surround and give meaning to the actions of political leaders. It does so by taking communication seriously: especially the discourses, images, and public arts that constitute collective identity and public opinion. These can be analysed not merely to identify self-interest and perceptions of power and balance, but also to identify multiple other drivers of political action (cf. Rice 2008).

These extended — but not extrinsic — elements of consciousness are evident in the self-definition and scope of ISIS. The organisation invests heavily not only in military but also in media operations. It threatens others not only by territorial conquest, but also through its persuasive reach across continents to hundreds of millions of followers. It is also an economic actor, supervising commercial activity in the sectors that it controls, profiting from a range of industries from oil to drugs, paying its civil servants and soldiers, though not always well. ISIS is finally a social, cultural, and theological actor. It aims at 'the restoration of an Islamic golden age and a "glorious" new caliphate based on holy war' (Harris, 2014).

More than Military Actions

Post-realism, like realism, includes military actions and war. In an anarchic world, violent capabilities are unevenly distributed and there is no universally accepted legitimate political order, no central authority, no governmental monopoly of violence. Force remains a powerful instrument of foreign policy, and ISIS certainly undertakes many military actions that are consistent with the standard realist narrative. Its massed attacks have seized and held territory such as Mosul in Iraq and al-Raqqah in Syria, at least temporarily. Its suicide bombers recall the Japanese kamikaze pilots of World War II. The Western response to ISIS' use of force also has had a strong military component, including advisors, special forces, drone strikes, conventional air and missile bombardment, and military assistance to allied groups. In domestic settings, standard and special police, counterinsurgency, and intelligence units have conducted operations with varying degrees of armed physical force (see, for example, Hayden 2016).

For post-realists, as for realists, military action does not exist for its own sake, but is necessarily embedded in a larger political context. In the formulation of the Prussian strategist Carl von Clausewitz (1984, 87), war is not 'a mere act of policy but a true political instrument, a continuation of political activity by other means.' Post-realism embraces a complex politics with a three-tiered model of strategic analysis and political management. First, leaders must compete and cooperate with other political actors to achieve their aims. Second, they must also maintain self-control, managing their own political reputations and identities before many different audiences. Third, leaders must juggle multiple incommensurable political discourses to balance and attain their diverse objectives (Beer and Hariman 1996, 387-414).

Post-realism includes more than military actions. Hard and soft power coexist inside a wider envelope of smart power. The leader's toolbox includes not only conflict but also cooperation, not only physical but also verbal behaviour. Post-realism recognises the need to adapt to the evolving political, economic, social, and technological complexities of asymmetric interaction in physical and media environments, and in cyberspace. A wide variety of modalities — military, political, diplomatic, economic, communicative, rhetorical, and cultural — are available for use.

Diplomacy and Politics

Post-realism follows realism in accepting the unavoidable existence of carefully modulated and targeted military force in dealing with ISIS. But, as Hans Morgenthau long ago emphasised, diplomacy also remains essential in mobilising allies with common interests and values in the Western and Arab worlds. Post-realism follows this thread, but goes beyond it; to state diplomacy, it adds public diplomacy.

Post-realism also asks how the fundamental assumptions of military and political action may be changing. Military action itself has increasingly become a form of politics. As Simpson (2013, 1, 230, 243–4) suggests, war is increasingly a military political hybrid. 'The use of armed force,' he says, 'seeks to establish military conditions for a political solution.' At the same time, armed force 'directly seeks political, as opposed to specifically military, outcomes.' War is less compartmentalised than it used to be. It is 'increasingly merging [...] with regular political activity.' As 'operational military ideas are invested with policy-like quality, we are confronted with policy as an extension of war' rather than war as an extension of policy. War has become 'an interpretive structure, which makes war "itself" a particular political instrument. War offers an interpretive template which can be used [...] to persuade audiences to understand conflict in a [...] "military" way.' Thus, post-realism shifts from simple, reductive models of conflict to understanding that war and politics alike are structured by conflicting category interpretations.

Economics

Post-realism's concern with more than military actions certainly includes economic dimensions. In this, it follows traditional realism's concern with the economic bases of power. In the famous phrase from President Eisenhower's farewell address, the military-industrial complex functions as a blended unit. Economic capabilities seamlessly support military forces. In World War II, for example, American production lines became the 'arsenal of democracy.'

We have already referred to ISIS' range of revenue generating operations. ISIS receives contributions from religiously oriented actors. Further, ISIS is also a business conglomerate. Western military operations — for example, bombing oil facilities and supply lines under ISIS control — have aimed to degrade some of these activities. Beyond this, however, economic sanctions and embargoes have been an important tactical tool. Western domination of the global financial system has also restricted ISIS' capabilities.

A post-realist perspective also suggests the importance of economic incentives in attracting ISIS recruits. Slow and uneven economic development — limited growth and economic inequality — in many parts of the Islamic and Western worlds has left behind a huge mass of unemployed youth susceptible to *jihadi* appeals. *Jihad* is, among other things, a jobs program. Like the Western military, it sucks up unemployed youth, providing economic opportunity, group solidarity, and a mission. Parts of the mission evolve in lands directly under ISIS control; other operations occur in third world or Western territories. No Western strategy for dealing with ISIS can possibly succeed over the long term without serious attention to economic growth and employment — particularly youth employment in Islamic, developing, and Western worlds.

Communication and Rhetoric

Post-realism, as a variant of realism, has a distinctive focus on communication and rhetoric (cf. Pinkerton 2011; Der Derian 2009; Hanson 2008). It strongly suggests that realism is limited theoretically and strategically by inattention to discourse, not least its own rhetorical habits. All global actors, including realists, are also rhetorical actors engaged in constant communication with each other. Military success will have limited value and duration unless the many negotiations of cultural identity in the region are addressed, and addressed while being well aware of the cultural and rhetorical problems confronting any reassertion of Western norms. Talk is not cheap.

ISIS is a rhetorical actor and a sophisticated user of social media. Its messaging is highly structured, though subtly differentiated from other groups like al-Qaeda. In a standard militant propaganda script, the enemy is strong, numerous, homogeneous, evil and must be defeated. ISIS suffers tremendously from the enemy in spite of the fact that its leaders and members are virtuous, united, and pure. ISIS can hurt and defeat the enemy by strict religious observance, unity, and violence (see Cohen et al. 2016). ISIS also has its own rhetorical sensitivities. Nance (2016, 428) suggests that 'there are some words that they really hate.' In particular, they abhor the name *Khawarij*, which is the name of 'the first Islamic cult group that the Prophet Mohammed warned against.' And they have rhetorical weaknesses: ISIS has been less successful than some of its competitors in adapting to local vernaculars and pushing a persuasive discourse to specific audiences. Speaking of al-Qaeda in the Arabian Peninsula, Elisabeth Kendall (2015) suggests that:

> AQAP's staying power is explained, at least in part, by its production of jihadist narratives that are culturally attuned to their Yemeni context and adapted to prevailing local conditions. ISIS, by contrast, has produced little narrative [...] that is culturally specific to Yemen beyond savaging the Houthis, tribesmen from Yemen's north who swept down through Yemen's south in 2015.

That said, ISIS also employs powerful rhetorical devices, globally broadcasting its ideology and its actions to promulgate its message and attract its followers.

Culture

Post-realism also emphasises the importance of culture. The communicative prowess of ISIS becomes apparent by considering how it is a cultural actor. There are many organisations that offer jobs, social services, and military adventure, but ISIS more than others has forged a transnational, militant, Islamic ideology that has been able to disrupt state and tribal regimes, consolidate and project power, and dominate Western perception of the region. They do so through consistent assertion of a worldview that is irredentist, theocratic, and absolutist, thereby directly tapping the *ressentiment* produced by the failures of modern state-building, secularism, and liberalism in the Middle East. The cultural contestation goes beyond interest to deeper questions of identity and legitimacy, and it goes beyond an analytics of power to turn on images of revenge and visions of the future. The cultural debates occur through words and images across a full range of communication media. These media practices depend on military success but also exceed the scope and outcomes of the battlefield.

Radical Islam pits the *dar al-Islam*, the house of Islam, against the territory of chaos or war. The leading realist of our time, Henry Kissinger, suggests that one of the main global tensions is the conflict between radical Islam, based on this vision, and the Westphalian state-based structure of world order. The continuing viability of the existing state system, in his view, depends on more than the material power of state elites. As the collapse of American foreign policy in Vietnam clearly showed, the exercise of power ultimately depends on the domestic and global legitimacy on which it is perceived to rest. 'To strike a balance between the two aspects of order — power and legitimacy,' Kissinger (2014, 367, 371) says, 'is the essence of statesmanship.'

Post-realism follows this realist concern and expands it. ISIS simultaneously appears as radically illegitimate within the Western cultural system while also confronting the legitimacy of the system itself. Western leaders must simultaneously oppose ISIS within the existing political order while also defending its cultural values. The apparent illegitimacy of ISIS helps leaders to mobilise popular opposition to it. At the same time, ISIS' outlaw status reduces its legibility for outsiders and diminishes the ability of Western leaders to analyse and negotiate interactions short of war. Nuanced Western responses can be perceived as liberal weakness; excessive reactions as imperial hypocrisy and overreach. Post-realism's strategic emphasis on balancing conflict and cooperation, self-presentation, and incommensurable interpretations illuminates the deep cultural tensions embedded in such legitimation conflicts and the delicacy of responding to them.

Responding to ISIS

Post-realism has a wider-angle lens than realism — including more actors than states, more motivations than interest and power, more actions than military deeds and war. It suggests several additional points of departure for response to the challenge that ISIS poses. These ideas hardly begin to sample possible reactions to ISIS, nor are they unique to post-realism; but they serve as examples of themes that can make more sense when anchored by the conventions of realist analysis and framed alongside them to address circumstances in the 21st century political environment. They include minimising strategic entrapment, developing wider countervailing alliances, and nurturing global civil society and economic development. Finally, they involve opening geographical space to go beyond existing territorial boundaries and opening theoretical space to go beyond realism.

Minimising Strategic Entrapment

Post-realism is concerned with minimising strategic entrapment. ISIS' strategy depends in part on drawing actors into traps, particularly military and rhetorical traps. In either case, extended war becomes more likely: the dynamic of stimulus, response, and escalation suggests caution lest the 'clash of civilisations' take extreme military form. Western framing of the 'global war on terror' or the 'long war' shows that the process of strategic entrapment is already well underway (Bacevich 2016; Doran 2016).

The sharpest provocations are ISIS' savage terrorist assaults on civilians. Journalists accustomed to battlefield immunity are captured and beheaded. Cities that surrender are offered draconian choices. Western states are targeted by terrorists and baited into disproportionate military reprisals. Western electorates under attack become frustrated and fearful, creating opportunities for politicians to make racist statements about all Muslims. Western political and moral assumptions seem no longer to apply.

Although elite analysts are of course aware of these dangers, they may not recognise specific susceptibilities to entrapment in muscular realism. Western political leaders are tempted to respond to ISIS' violent assaults with hard military and police power — iron fists with or without velvet gloves. When bombs or bombers explode, and both domestic and international audiences clamour for a response, realist scripts are activated, and can-do military solutions are easily oversold. The clamour for 'boots on the ground' can soon lead to a large occupying force, which is exactly what ISIS and similar groups would want. Occupation confirms every claim being made about the continued domination of the region by imperial powers enforcing a corrupt and corrupting Western civilisation.

A related temptation is to rationalise invasion and occupation with a familiar realist story line: that current political disorder is due to the imprudent actions of idealists (e.g., policy makers who mistakenly thought that they could create a stable democratic Iraq). This narrative plays into the hands of ISIS by ignoring cultural analysis and accommodation. Reactivating the realist-idealist framework makes it likely that policy makers will become mired in the assumptions of a militaristic realism that would make ISIS stronger, not weaker.

Developing Alliances and Wider Networks

Realists rightly emphasise that the management of power depends on both self-restraint and building alliances with others. Post-realism extends the strong tradition in realist theory toward limits and balancing commitments and capabilities in the support of core interests. Military operations are not likely to produce lasting gains otherwise, while alliance reliability depends on granular assessment of all the actors in particular locales. Post-realism confirms the realist's emphasis of analysing all parties in terms of self-interest and power while recognising that self-interest, cultural identity, and power itself are malleable factors within any specific situation.

Alliance building as a force multiplier has been an important element of realist theory and has been effective in rolling back ISIS territorial gains. This is true, not only in the obvious case of Western state cooperation in the North Atlantic Treaty Organisation (see Beer 2013), but also with non-Western states in regional and local contexts. Alliance development, however, necessarily goes beyond state cooperation, as military strategies that rely primarily on special forces and advisors require more, not less, interaction with non-state actors. Post-realism emphasises that alliance building requires also working with ethnic, tribal, and religious networks; with NGOs and other actors invested in the region; and with professional knowledge communities to coordinate broad-spectrum resistance to ISIS.

An additional consideration is that ISIS is not disposed toward a politics of alliance building. Their publication *Dabiq*, for example, reveals the weakness of absolutism: it sees far more enemies than friends. Likewise, captive populations are offered only complete ideological capitulation or death; the choice is obvious for most, but also one that depends almost entirely on continued military occupation. ISIS seems to be playing an all-or-nothing game, and in a region and at a time when weak states encourage resurgent identities and local autonomy. In that situation, a new imperial super-state such as a Caliphate is one possibility, but productive alliance building with many different groups for mutual benefits may be harder for ISIS than for many of its opponents.

Nurturing Global Civil Society

Consistent with certain strains of realism focusing on anarchical society, found in the English school of International Relations theory (see e.g. Murray 2016; Bull 2012; Manning 1975), we have emphasised a post-realist concern with moving from international disorder to globalising networks: cultivating diplomacy, politics, economic development, communication, and culture. Post-realism also stresses the major importance of nurturing civil society as a response to ISIS and a pathway to finding wider forms of possible attraction and assimilation in an evolving global community.

It seems clear from both its publications and occupying practices that ISIS is dedicated to the destruction of civil society — or at least the liberal democratic civil society that now is established or developing across much of the globe. This is the society of global news media, entertainment, and advertising; of market economics, uniform transportation technologies, and globalised cultures of consumption, and also rule of law, individual liberty, and tolerant civic habits. It is the most direct threat to ISIS, and its central target: first, in the region, but elsewhere as well, as when terrorist actions can degrade social trust, civic habits, and political discourse in Europe and the US. A commitment to the defence of civil society has to be undertaken with care, however, as the same cultural habitus comes with all the baggage of colonial domination, economic exploitation, and assertions of cultural superiority, as well as the destruction of traditional cultures still vitally important in daily life. The post-realist emphasis on reflexive analysis applies directly here.

The focus on civil society encompasses several other post-realist themes that are also relevant to the struggle against ISIS. The distinction between inside/outside, the domestic and the international sphere, obviously is set aside not due to an idealist temperament, but for strategic reasons. Across national boundaries, economic development and corresponding social justice concerns become crucial - and a potential advantage against an adversary whose primary economic opportunity is military service. Although economic progress is not a complete solution, it is essential.

Also important is the reaffirmation of the importance of moral norms in the global environment. The mobilisation against ISIS was provoked not only by its military success but rather by their dramatic overturning of modern conceptions of punishment and human rights. Modern regimes are not innocent, but public celebrations of crucifixion and immolation, and explicit defences of sexual slavery, pitch everyone into a radically different, catastrophically pre-modern world. The choice for Western policy makers at that point is at once clear and dangerous. It is clear, because norms are now both salient and powerful means for mobilising the necessary response. It is dangerous, because they can become a trap: an inducement to arrogant, ignorant, overly instrumental and militarised responses sure to provoke uncontrollable blowback. A defence of human rights should not become a license for counterproductive actions.

Opening Theoretical and Geographical Space

Finally, post-realism includes a concern with mentalities beyond national interest and power, indeed beyond realism itself. The response to ISIS could include recognition of what it has forced at great human cost, which is to create an open space for the political imagination. In a region where territorial boundaries seemed both fixed and hopelessly contested, and thus doomed to the stasis of perpetual hostility and hobbled development, ISIS — in realist terms — is a radical revisionist actor. It has shown that another and very different theoretical and geographical map, a new emergent pattern, is at least thinkable.

ISIS has revealed that a productive stability probably needs more than the brokering of existing national interests by outside powers and local elites. This awakening has been purchased at a horrific price — and made worse by the fact that it was unnecessary, had others been willing to do more than manage an impoverished status quo. The vision of modernisation had died — in both its Soviet and American emplotments — but all that had replaced it was the calculation of interests and balancing of power. That is not enough. It never was, nor will be.

References

Bacevich, Andrew J. 2016. *America's War for the Greater Middle East: A Military History*. New York: Random House.

Beer, Francis A. 2013. "NATO Now and Then: Alliance Agents and Structures in Anarchical International Society." *E-International Relations*, 27 August. (http://www.e-ir.info/2013/08/27/nato-now-and-then-alliance-agents-and-structures-in-anarchical-international-society/ accessed 21 August 2017)

Beer, Francis A. and Robert Hariman (eds). 1996. *Post-realism: The rhetorical turn in international relations*. East Lansing: Michigan State University Press.

Beer, Francis A. and Robert Hariman 2004. "Le post-réalisme après le 11 septembre", *Études Internationales* 35(4): 689–719.

Bew, John. 2015. *Realpolitik: A History.* New York: Oxford University Press.

Bull, Hedley. 2012. *The Anarchical Society: A study of order in world politics.* 4th ed. New York: Columbia University Press.

Clausewitz, Carl von. 1984. *On War.* Edited and translated by Michael Howard and Peter Paret. Princeton: Princeton University Press.

Cohen, Shuki J., Arie Kruglanski, Michele J. Gelfand, David Webber, and Rohan Gunaratna. 2016. "Al-Qaeda's propaganda decoded: A psycholinguistic system for detecting variations in terrorism ideology." *Terrorism and Political Violence* 5(9): 1–30.

Cross, Mai'a K. D. 2013. *Security Integration in Europe: How Knowledge-based Networks Are Transforming the European Union.* Ann Arbor: University of Michigan Press.

Der Derian, James. 2009. *Virtuous War: Mapping The Military-industrial-media-entertainment Network.* 2nd edition. New York: Routledge.

Doran, Michael. 2016. *Ike's Gamble: America's Rise to Dominance in the Middle East.* New York: Free Press.

Elman, Colin and Michael Jensen (eds). 2014. *The realism reader.* 1st edition. London: Routledge.

Gerges, Fawaz A. 2016. *ISIS: A History.* Princeton: Princeton University Press.

Haas, Ernst B. 1991. *When Knowledge is Power: Three Models of Change in International Organizations.* Berkeley: University of California Press.

Hanson, Elizabeth C. 2008. *The Information Revolution and World Politics.* London: Rowman and Littlefield.

Harris, David. 2014. "The Islamic State's (ISIS, ISIL) Magazine." *Clarion Project.* (http://www.clarionproject.org/news/islamic-state-isis-isil-propaganda-magazine-dabiq accessed 10 September 2016)

Hayden, Michael V. 2016. *Playing to the Edge: American Intelligence in the Age of Terror*. New York: Penguin.

Kendall, Elisabeth. 2015. "Al-Qa'ida & Islamic state in Yemen: A battle for local audiences". (https://www.academia.edu/15757466/Al-Qaida_and_Islamic_State_in_Yemen_A_Battle_for_Local_Audiences accessed 21 August 2017)

Kissinger, Henry. 2014. *World Order*. New York: Penguin.

Legro, Jeffrey W. and Andrew Moravcsik. 1999. "Is Anybody Still a Realist?" *International Security* 24(2): 5–55.

Manning, C. A. W. 1975. *The Nature of International Society*. London: Macmillan.

Murray, Robert W. (ed). 2016. *System, Society & the World: Exploring the English School of International Relations*. 2nd edition. Bristol: E-International Relations Publishing.

Nance, Malcolm. 2016. *Defeating ISIS: Who They Are, How They Fight, What They Believe.* New York: Skyhorse.

Pinkerton, Alasdair. 2011. "Weapons of mass communication: The securitization of social networking sites." *Political Geography* 30: 115–117.

Rice, Condoleeza. 2008. "Rethinking the National Interest - American Realism for a New World." *Foreign Affairs,* July/August.

Simpson, Emile. 2013. *War From the Ground Up: Twenty-First Century Combat as Politics*. Oxford: Oxford University Press.

3

The Past, Present and Future of Realism

ARASH HEYDARIAN PASHAKHANLOU

Structural realism or neorealism seeks to explain International Relations on the basis of the structural pressures induced by anarchy. Structural realists, however, differ in their assessment of how much power states require under these conditions. For this reason, neorealism is often divided into two sub branches: defensive and offensive realism. Defensive realism contends that states should acquire an appropriate amount of power necessary for them to thrive. They should however not maximise their relative power in a quest to become hegemons.[1] Such a behaviour is deemed counterproductive as it will provoke the formation of an opposing coalition that will undermine their position (Grieco 1988; Mastanduno 1997, 79 n. 13; Waltz 1988; Waltz 2008, 79). In contrast, offensive realism maintains that states should maximise their relative power to become hegemons, if they have the opportunity to do so. In this view, power preponderance is the best safeguard for states' survival (Labs 1997; Layne 2000, 106; Mearsheimer 2010, 78).

The leading proponent of defensive realism, Kenneth Waltz, and the most influential advocate of offensive realism, John Mearsheimer, both maintain that their respective theories continue to be the most powerful lenses for understanding international politics in the post-Cold War world (Waltz 1997, 916; Waltz 2004, 6; Mearsheimer 2001, 168, 361). The present chapter will put this proposition to test by evaluating the merits of Waltz's defensive

---

[1]   Kenneth Waltz's defensive realism only considers global hegemony where there is only one great power in the international system. Under such conditions, the international system is said to be unipolar as there are no other 'poles' or states that can balance the power of the hegemon. John Mearsheimer's offensive realism however makes a distinction between global and regional hegemons. The former dominate the entire planet while the latter rules over a continent (Mearsheimer 2001, 40).

realism and Mearsheimer's offensive realism in this new order where the United States has clearly emerged as the leading power (Pashakhanlou 2009; Pashakhanlou 2013; Pashakhanlou 2014; Pashakhanlou 2016).[2] Specifically, this chapter will examine the theories of Waltz and Mearsheimer against their own empirical analysis of the post-Cold War era to verify whether they can account for contemporary international relations.

The result of this inquiry indicates that none of these theories could have had any explanatory power in the post-Cold War world, if assessed on their own terms. This is because neither Waltz's defensive realism nor Mearsheimer's offensive realism is equipped to account for interstate relations under hegemony[3] and unipolarity[4], a condition which both scholars argue has characterised the international system with the ascendency of the United States after the end of the Cold War in their later writings.

This argument is advanced over the remainder of this chapter. The first section explains how the theories of Waltz and Mearsheimer will be assessed and highlights the utility of this approach. The second section is dedicated to the defensive realism of Waltz. Here, his theory is outlined along with his empirical analysis of the post-Cold War world. The inability of Waltz's defensive realism to account for international politics under hegemony and unipolarity are also highlighted here. The ensuing section is devoted to the offensive realism of Mearsheimer. This segment provides an overview of his offensive realism, empirical assessment of the post-Cold War era and an explanation of why hegemony and unipolarity invariably create anomalies for his theory. A conclusion that briefly summarises the preceding points and argues for the need of new theories of international politics brings this chapter to a closure. At this point, it is however appropriate to take a closer look at how the defensive and offensive realism of Waltz and Mearsheimer will be assessed.

---

[2]   Although there has been a debate on whether the post-Cold War world has been unipolar, multipolar or something else, there is a widespread agreement that the United States has been the most powerful state in the international system ever since the fall of the Soviet Union.

[3]   As has been noted, Mearsheimer's offensive realism makes a distinction between regional and global hegemony. In the former case, only the region dominated by a hegemon becomes an anomaly to Mearsheimer's theory. In the presence of a global hegemon, the entire world however becomes incomprehensible to his offensive realism. Since Waltz's defensive realism only considers global hegemony, the entire international system becomes an anomaly to his theory in the presence of a hegemon.

[4]   As will be demonstrated, the enduring features of the international system (such as anarchy) are not enough to save either Waltz's defensive realism or Mearsheimer's offensive realism. Hegemony and unipolarity pose inherent difficulties for both theories that make them defunct irrespective of other structural features of the system.

Theory Assessment

First, as has already been mentioned, this investigation puts to test what Waltz and Mearsheimer themselves claim for their theory – that their theories still retain their explanatory power in the post-Cold War era. The great advantage of this approach is that it can no longer be claimed that the criteria for evaluation is not suitable for the theories in question as could have been the case if the theories would have been examined against externally derived criteria from the works of Karl Popper, Imre Lakatos, Thomas Kuhn, etc. (see Jackson and Nexon 2009; Moravcsik 2003 and Waltz 1997).

Second, the current investigation examines defensive and offensive realism as presented by Waltz and Mearsheimer and does not treat these two distinct realist theories as a monolithic block under the broad banner of 'realism' or 'neorealism' under the illusion that they are somehow equivalent to one another, which is a rather common practice in the discipline of IR. As William Wohlforth (2008, 131 and 143) rightly points out, to reduce the realist school of thought 'to a single, internally consistent, and logically coherent theory is the taproot of the greatest misunderstanding'; studies that do so generate 'profoundly misleading' results.

Third, the explanatory power of both theories are evaluated against Waltz's and Mearsheimer's own empirical analysis of the post-Cold War world rather than my own interpretation of this era or that of others. Altogether, this evaluation of the explanatory power of Waltz's defensive realism and Mearsheimer's offensive realism presents an easy test for their theories. This is evident as they are evaluated against the principles of the theorists themselves and their own empirical analysis of the post-Cold War era. If the theories cannot pass such an easy test, their validity is seriously called into question (George and Bennett 2005, 122). With that said, we can now turn our attention to the theories themselves, starting with Waltz's defensive realism.

Waltz's Defensive Realism in the Post-Cold War World

Waltz's defensive realism[5] offers a systemic and state-centric theory of international politics. The structural components of Waltz's defensive realism consist of anarchy defined as the absence of government and the distribution of capabilities across the system. In doing so, Waltz strips away other features of the international order and every attribute of states except their

---

[5]   For other influential defensive realist statements, see for example Jervis 1976; Walt 1987; Snyder 1991.

capabilities from his theory (Waltz 1979, 99). Moreover, Waltz (1979, 91–2, 118–9) only makes two explicit assumptions regarding states: that they are unitary actors and that they, at minimum, pursue policies to ensure their own survival.

Since Waltz (1979, 105, 118) assumes that states are unitary actors that only differ in their capabilities and have to take care of themselves in the anarchic system, the balance of power becomes an 'iron law' as states can only assure their survival by making sure that none of their rivals grow too powerful. The balance of power is the dynamic part of Waltz's otherwise static theoretical model as he contends that the number of great powers, who possess the greatest capabilities, makes up the balance or the poles of the international system and shape its character (1979, 129–130, 144). In this regard, the differentiations are between a bipolar system where the balance is maintained by two great powers and a multipolar system in which the anarchic system is inhabited by three or more great powers (Waltz 1979, 161). In Waltz's view, a bipolar world is more stable than a multipolar world since 'uncertainties about who threatens whom, about who will oppose whom, and about who will gain or lose from the actions of other states accelerate as the number of states increases' (1979, 165).

Interestingly, Waltz makes no mention of unipolarity in his highly influential 1979 monograph, *Theory of International Politics.* In his empirical writings and his publications after 1993, Waltz has however consistently maintained that the post-Cold War world is unipolar with the United States as the reigning hegemon (see e.g. Waltz 1997, 914; Waltz 2000a, 27; Waltz 2000b, 23; Waltz 2004, 4–6). In his article *Structural Realism after the Cold War* published at the dawn of the new millennium, Waltz for instance writes that '[u]pon the demise of the Soviet Union, the international political system became unipolar' (2000b, 27). Although Waltz has constantly claimed that the post-Cold War era has been characterised by unipolarity and global American hegemony in his publications published after 'The Emerging Structure of International Politics', he has insisted that the unipolar moment will be brief and that the world will eventually become multipolar (Waltz 2000b, 29–41; Waltz 2000a, 25–36).

It is not hard to see why Waltz consistently points out that unipolarity will be short-lived and that the world will become multipolar in the future. His theory does, after all, assume that states will balance against a preponderant power no matter how benign the hegemon might be (Waltz 2000b, 30). Consequently, Waltz (2000b, 30, 36–8) maintains that American power will be checked in the blink of an eye, historically speaking. Waltz (2000b, 36–8) is also careful to point out that the United States cannot do anything to solidify its hegemony, as a new balancing coalition will be formed against it, no matter what measures the US takes to prevent such an outcome.[6] Waltz himself specifically acknowledges that the balancing principle that his theory is based on suggests that American hegemony and unipolarity will be replaced by a multipolar system (2000b, 30). Waltz asserts that the European Union or a German-led coalition, China, Japan, and in a more distant future Russia will be the most likely balancers in this new constellation.

At this point, many eyebrows may be raised concerning Waltz's treatment of unipolarity and multipolarity. As Richard Little (2007, 189) puts it: '[g]iven the significance that Waltz attaches to the economics analogy and the importance that economists attach to monopoly, the failure to open up the issue of unipolarity in *Theory of International Politics* is surprising, while the focus on multipolarity in the post-Cold War era becomes distinctly odd.' This omission of unipolarity and emphasis on multipolarity is however fully understandable once one realises that unipolarity is a condition that Waltz's theory is inherently unable to deal with.

As has been mentioned, his defensive realism is a state-centric systemic theory of international politics based on the anarchic structure of the international system and the distribution of capabilities across the system that revolves around balance of power which can be either bipolar or multipolar, according to Waltz's writings in *Theory of International Politics*. In an anarchic unipolar world, there are however no longer any systemic constraints to shove and shape the hegemon's behaviour in the international system. After all, Waltz maintains that states are judges in their own cases in an anarchic system (1959, 159). This means that even though anarchy may still persist in Waltz's post-Cold War world, it can by itself not constrain the behaviour of the hegemon. Indeed, the hegemon can do as it pleases in the absence of a global Leviathan. This is because there is by definition no other greater power to balance against the hegemon in a unipolar world in order to constrain its behaviour. Hence, the necessary structural constraints that Waltz relies upon to explain state behaviour are no longer at play concerning the hegemon in unipolarity (2000b, 27).

Even Waltz implicitly acknowledges this fact in a passage when he writes that: '[t]hrough the long years of the Cold War the might of each superpower

---

[6]   In this regard, Waltz writes: 'the task will exceed America's economic, military, demographic, and political resources; and the very effort to maintain a hegemonic position is the surest way to undermine it. The effort to maintain dominance stimulates some countries to work to overcome it (2000b, 38).' Waltz also notes that '[t]he United States cannot prevent a new balance of power from forming. It can hasten its coming as it has been earnestly doing.' (2000b, 36–7)'

balanced the might of the other and moderated the behaviour of both of them. Now the only superpower left in the field is free to act on its whims and follow its fancies' (2004, 5). Waltz goes on to postulate that in a unipolar world there are no longer any checks and balances on the hegemon. Its behaviour is instead determined by its own internal policies rather than external structural pressures (Waltz 2003, 5).

This revelation suggests that Waltz's (2004, 3) theory that 'explains how external forces shape states' behaviour, but says nothing about the effects of internal forces' as he himself points out, cannot account for the hegemon in unipolarity. If we consider Waltz's own arguments – that a) there are hardly any external forces on the hegemon in a unipolarity and that its behaviour is instead determined by its own internal forces and b) that his defensive realism can only explain how external forces affect state behaviour and have nothing to say about the effects of internal forces, the only conclusion that can be drawn is that his theory is inherently unequipped to account for the behaviour of the hegemon.

It is also important to note that it is not only the behaviour of the sole great power in the international system – the hegemon – that becomes an anomaly to Waltz's defensive realism under unipolarity but the entire system as a whole. This is evident when Waltz maintains that: '[i]n systems theory, structure is a generative notion; and the structure of a system is generated by the interactions of its principal parts [the great power(s)]' as the 'fates of all the states ... are affected much more by the acts and the interactions of the major ones than of the minor ones' (1979, 72). For this reason, Waltz claims that his general theory of international politics is based on the great powers but applies to lesser states 'insofar as their interactions are insulated from the intervention of the great powers of a system' (Waltz 1979, 73).

Hence, since Waltz's theory is admittedly based on the great powers and can only account for the behaviour of other states in so far as they can be induced from that of the great power(s), it must consequently mean that his defensive realism cannot account for smaller states either in unipolarity as it is incapable of explaining the behaviour of the only great power in the system under these conditions. As such, Waltz's state-centric theory of international politics becomes inherently unable to account for any state behaviour under unipolarity. This is why the entire system becomes unexplainable by his theory. Indeed, since Waltz has argued that the international system has in fact been characterised by American hegemony since the end of the Cold War in his writings after 1993, this must mean that his theory cannot have had any explanatory power in the post-Cold War world, if assessed on its own terms.

In sum, the entire post-Cold War period has thus far been anomalous to Waltz's defensive realism and it has been unable to account for what it is designed to do: explain 'international outcomes' or 'a small number of big and important things' (Waltz 1986, 329; Waltz 1996, 54–7).

Mearsheimer's Offensive Realism in the Post-Cold War World

Mearsheimer's offensive realism[7] is also a structural theory of international politics that affords special attention to great powers, but claims to have relevance for other states as well to varying degrees (Mearsheimer 2001, 17–22, 403 n. 5). Just like Waltz's defensive realism, the offensive realism of Mearsheimer also assumes that the international system is anarchic where survival is the main objective of states (2001, 29–32). Mearsheimer however adds three additional assumptions to his theory that are not among Waltz's explicit assumptions. Mearsheimer's three additional explicit assumptions are as follows:

1. States always possess an offensive capability, which enables them to hurt and potentially destroy one another.
2. International relations take place in the existential condition of uncertainty, making assessments regarding others' intentions with absolute certainty impossible. Consequently, no state can be fully assured that its rivals will not turn their military apparatus against it at any given time.
3. States are rational actors (Mearsheimer 2001, 30–1).

Mearsheimer contends that the combination of all his five assumptions pushes states to maximise their relative power as opposed to seeking an 'appropriate' amount of power as in Waltz's defensive realism (Waltz 1979; Waltz 1988, 616–7; Mearsheimer 2001, 30–1). As such, all great powers aspire to reach the pinnacle of power, hegemony. In stark contrast to Waltz's defensive realism, which only considers global hegemony, Mearsheimer's offensive realism however makes a distinction between global hegemons and regional hegemons (2001, 40). The former dominates the entire planet while the latter rules over a continent. Offensive realism maintains that a state has to enjoy military superiority and be the only great power in the international system to qualify as a hegemon (Mearsheimer 2001, 40).

Offensive realism can, however, not explain international politics under the condition of hegemony. Mearsheimer makes this point clear when he writes that; '[i]f one state achieves hegemony, the system ceases to be anarchic and

---

[7]   For other offensive realist publications, see for example Elman 2004; Labs 1997; Layne 2000.

becomes hierarchic. Offensive realism, which assumes international anarchy, has little to say about politics under hierarchy. Thus, realism is likely to provide important insights about world politics for the foreseeable future, save for what goes on inside in a region that is dominated by a hegemon' (Mearsheimer 2001, 415 n. 13).[8] In his earlier empirical assessments, Mearsheimer only contends that the Western Hemisphere and Western Europe have been hierarchic. Indeed, Mearsheimer (2001, 40–1, 239) asserts that the United States has been the regional hegemon of a hierarchic Western Hemisphere since at least 1900. Concerning Western Europe, Mearsheimer (2001, 529 n. 63) insists that the large American presence in this area since World War II has made the region hierarchic rather than anarchic.

If we add up Mearsheimer's own two assertions; (1) that offensive realism is unable to account for international politics under hegemony since it makes the relationship within that region hierarchic and (2) that the Western Hemisphere has been hierarchic since at least 1900 and Western Europe from 1945 and onwards, this must consequently mean that offensive realism has been unable to explain foreign policy behaviour and international outcomes within these regions from these dates onwards. These anomalies will also persist as long as they remain hierarchic.

In his earlier work prior to 2012, Mearsheimer does however not acknowledge that the United States has been the global hegemon. It can thus not be argued that offensive realism has been unable to explain the entire world on basis of these writings. In these publications, Mearsheimer (2001, 40, 141, 381) maintains that the post-Cold War era has been multipolar rather than unipolar, with the United States, China and Russia as the great powers. This assertion however creates major inconsistencies between Mearsheimer's theoretical and empirical analysis of international politics.

First, Mearsheimer posits that a state must have the military might 'to put up a serious fight against' the most formidable power in the international system to qualify as a great power (2001, 40, 528 n. 60). Mearsheimer however claims that the main competitor of the United States in the post-Cold World, China, 'does not possess a formidable military today and it is certainly in no position to pick a fight with the United States ... even in the Asia-Pacific region' (2010, 384–5). As such, Mearsheimer's own empirical analysis suggests that China does not satisfy offensive realism's defining criterion of a great power. If China cannot be regarded as a great power, then neither can Russia, since Mearsheimer considers Russia as the weaker of the two (2006, 119–120).

---

[8]   For a different conception of anarchy and hierarchy than that offered by Mearsheimer's offensive realism, see for example Donnelly 2006; Lake 2009.

Second, if the United States is merely a regional rather than a global hegemon, then it should essentially behave as a status-quo power and an offshore balancer in other parts of the world, unless its exalted position becomes threatened by an aspiring potential hegemon, according to the offensive realism of Mearsheimer (2001, 141). In his 2011 article 'Imperial by Design', Mearsheimer himself however makes it clear that this is not the way the United States has behaved in the post-Cold War era. Instead of acting as an offshore balancer in other parts of the world, Mearsheimer contends that America has adopted 'a flawed grand strategy' aimed at global domination (2011, 18). Under such conditions, Mearsheimer's offensive realism also expects the other great powers in the system, China and Russia, to balance against the aggressor (2001, 45). Yet, Mearsheimer (2001, 528 n. 62) explicitly contends that no serious balancing coalition has been formed or is likely to be formed against the United States.

The only explanation that could account for these major discrepancies between Mearsheimer's theoretical and empirical analysis of international politics is that the United States is the sole great power in the international system and that the post-Cold War world has been unipolar rather than multipolar. This could explain why the US has managed to dominate the world and the reason why China and Russia have not balanced against the United States. For these reasons, it is not hard to see why even Mearsheimer has endorsed the view that America is the global hegemon on numerous occasions from 2012 and onwards. This is apparent when Mearsheimer (2012, 5–6, emphasis added) suggests that

> [w]hat's happened over the past 23 years [after the end of the Cold War in 1989] is that the distribution of power—call it *unipolarity*, American primacy, or whatever you want—has left the US free to misbehave... A world with the Soviet Union or its equivalent is fundamentally different from the post-Cold War world. As I said before, the architecture of the system doesn't discipline the US anymore. So, it's free to run around the world doing all sorts of foolish things.

In his 2013 piece, co-authored with Stephen Walt, Mearsheimer again reaffirms that he considers the current international system unipolar. This is evident when Mearsheimer and Walt write that the 'advent of *unipolarity* requires us to devise new theories to explain how this new configuration of power will affect world politics' (2013, 437, emphasis added). At another passage of the paper, they contend that: 'one cannot be sure that a new grand theory or a powerful middle-range theory will not be created, especially given the emergence of new political conditions (e.g. *unipolarity*, globalisation, etc.) that we want to understand' (Mearsheimer and Walt 2013, 445, emphasis added). Mearsheimer expresses the same view in his 2014 article *America Unhinged*. Here, he persists that the 'United States is a remarkably safe country, which is what allows it to behave foolishly without jeopardising its security. The *'unipolar moment,'* coupled with America's geographical location and nuclear arsenal, creates a permissive environment for irresponsible behaviour, which its leaders have been quick to exploit' (Mearsheimer 2014, 23, emphasis added).

As has been demonstrated, unipolarity means that the entire world becomes hierarchic by the standards of offensive realism, which is a condition that Mearsheimer himself acknowledges that his theory is unable to explain. This means that the offensive realism of Mearsheimer cannot have had any explanatory power at all in the post-Cold War world, if evaluated on its own terms.

Conclusion

This chapter has evaluated the explanatory power of the two main theories of structural realism, Waltz's defensive realism and Mearsheimer's offensive realism, in the post-Cold War world. The findings of this inquiry suggest that neither Waltz's defensive realism nor Mearsheimer's offensive realism could have had any explanatory power in the post-Cold War era, if assessed on their own terms. Indeed, both of these scholars have themselves acknowledged that the post-Cold War environment has been characterised by American hegemony and unipolarity, a condition which their structural realist theories are admittedly incapable to account for. It is thus clear that although both of these realist statements purport to focus on great power politics, they are ironically unable to explain international politics once a state reaches the pinnacle of power, hegemony, as the United States managed to do after the end of the Cold War according to both Waltz and Mearsheimer. The inability of these structural realist theories to shed light on international relations will also continue as long as unipolarity ensues. For these reasons, new general realist theories of international politics need to be developed that can succeed where the defensive realism of Waltz and the offensive realism of Mearsheimer have failed.

References

Donnelly, Jack. 2006. "Sovereign Inequalities and Hierarchy in Anarchy: American Power and International Society". *European Journal of International Relations* 12(2): 139–170.

Elman, Colin. 2004. "Extending Offensive Realism: The Louisiana Purchase and America's Rise to Regional Hegemony". *American Political Science Review* 98(4): 563–576.

George, Alexander and Andrew Bennett. 2005. *Case Studies and Theory Development in the Social Sciences.* Cambridge, MA: MIT Press.

Grieco, Joseph. 1988. "Anarchy and the Limits of Cooperation: A Realist Critique of the Newest Liberal Institutionalism". *International Organization* 42(3): 485–507.

Jackson, Patrick T. and Daniel Nexon. 2009. "Paradigmatic Faults in International Relations Theory". *International Studies Quarterly* 53(4): 907–930.

Jervis, Robert. 1976. *Perception and Misperception in International Politics.* Princeton: Princeton University Press.

Labs, Eric. 1997. "Beyond Victory: Offensive Realism and the Expansion of War Aims". *Security Studies* 6(4): 1–49.

Lake, David. 2009. *Hierarchy in International Relations.* Ithaca, NY: Cornell University Press.

Layne, Christopher. 2000. "From Preponderance to Offshore Balancing: America's Future Grand Strategy". *America's Strategic Choices*, edited by Michael Brown et al., 99–140. Cambridge, MA: MIT Press.

Layne, Christopher. 2002. "The 'Poster Child for Offensive Realism': America as a Global Hegemon". *Security Studies* 12(2): 120–164.

Little, Richard. 2007. *The Balance of Power in International Relations: Metaphors, Myths and Models.* Cambridge: Cambridge University Press.

Mastanduno, Michael. 1997. "Preserving the Unipolar Moment: Realist Theories and U.S. Grand Strategy after the Cold War". *International Security* 21(4): 49–88.

Mearsheimer, John. 2001. *The Tragedy of Great Power Politics.* New York: WW Norton and Company.

Mearsheimer, John. 2006. "Conversations in International Relations: Interview with John J. Mearsheimer (Part I)". *International Relations* 20(1): 105–123.

Mearsheimer, John. 2010. "Structural Realism". *International Relations Theories: Discipline and Diversity 2nd Edition*, edited by Tim Dunne, Milja Kurki and Steve Smith, 77–94. Oxford: Oxford University Press.

Mearsheimer, John. 2011. "Imperial by Design". *Foreign Affairs* 70(111): 16–34.

Mearsheimer, John. 2012. John Mearsheimer On Power as the Currency of International Relations, Disciplining US Foreign Policy, and Being an Independent Variable. (http://www.theory-talks.org/2012/06/theory-talk-49.html, Accessed on 21/05/2017)

Mearsheimer, John. 2014. "America Unhinged". *The National Interest*, 129: 9–30.

Mearsheimer, John and Stephen Walt. 2013. "Leaving Theory Behind: Why Simplistic Hypothesis Testing Is Bad for International Relations" *European Journal of International Relations* 19(3): 427–457.

Moravcsik, Andrew. 2003. "Liberal International Relations Theory: A Scientific Assessment". *Progress in International Relations Theory: Appraising the Field*, edited by Colin Elman and Miriam Elman, 159-204. Cambridge, MA: MIT Press.

Pashakhanlou, Arash Heydarian. 2009. "Comparing and Contrasting Classical Realism and Neorealism: A Re-Examination of Hans Morgenthau's and Kenneth Waltz's Theories of International Relations." (http://www.e-ir.info/2009/07/23/comparing-and-contrasting-classical-realism-and-neo-realism/ Accessed on 21/05/2017).

Pashakhanlou, Arash Heydarian. 2013. "Back to the Drawing Board: A Critique of Offensive Realism". *International Relations* 27(2): 202–225.

Pashakhanlou, Arash Heydarian. 2014. "Waltz, Mearsheimer and the Post-Cold War World: The Rise of America and the Fall of Structural Realism". *International Politics* 51(3): 295–315.

Pashakhanlou, Arash Heydarian. 2016. *Realism and Fear in International Relations: Morgenthau, Waltz and Mearsheimer Reconsidered*. London: Palgrave.

Snyder, Jack. 1991. *Myths of Empire: Domestic Politics and International Ambition*. Ithaca, NY: Cornell University Press.

Walt, Stephen. 1987. *The Origins of Alliances*. Ithaca, NY: Cornell University Press.

Waltz, Kenneth. 1959. *Man the State and War: A Theoretical Analysis*. New York: Columbia University Press.

Waltz, Kenneth. 1979. *Theory of International Politics*. New York: McGraw-Hill.

Waltz, Kenneth. 1986. "Reflections on Theory of International Politics: A Response to My Critics". In *Neorealism and Its Critics*, edited by Robert Keohane, 322–45. New York: Columbia University Press.

Waltz, Kenneth. 1988. "The Origins of War in Neorealist Theory". *Journal of Interdisciplinary History* 18(4): 615–628.

Waltz, Kenneth. 1996. "International Politics Is Not Foreign Policy". *Security Studies* 6(1): 54–57.

Waltz, Kenneth. 1997. "Evaluating Theories". *The American Political Science Review* 91(4): 913–917.

Waltz, Kenneth. 2000a. "NATO Expansion: A Realist's View". *Contemporary Security Policy* 21(2): 23–38.

Waltz, Kenneth. 2000b. "Structural Realism after the Cold War". *International Security* 25(1): 5–41.

Waltz, Kenneth. 2003. Conversations with Kenneth N. Waltz Ford Professor Emeritus of Political Science, UC Berkeley. (http://globetrotter.berkeley.edu/people3/Waltz/waltz-con0.html, accessed on 21/05/2017).

Waltz, Kenneth. 2004. "Neorealism: Confusions and Criticisms". *Journal of Politics & Society* 15(1): 2–6.

Waltz, Kenneth. 2008. *Realism and International Politics*. New York: Routledge.

Wohlforth, William. 2008. "Realism". In *The Oxford Handbook of International Relations*, edited by Christian Reus-Smit and Duncan Snidal, 131–49. Oxford: Oxford University Press.

4

When Hard Power Shrinks: The Midlife Crisis of Realism

TONY C. LEE

This chapter scrutinises the midlife crisis of realism through its most essential theoretic construct: power. Having identified several problems in realism's conception of power, I argue that the theory has lost its momentum as a dominant theory in international relations. This chapter starts by reviewing the concept of power advocated by several schools of realism. This review is followed by a critique exposing realism's major 'power issues.' The case of China is then analysed as it seems to particularly challenge the realist concept of power. The analysis leads to a discussion about the (uncertain) future of realism.

Realism on Power: A Brief Review

The history of realism is a portrayal of power. Thucydides (460–400 B.C.), the father of realism, had already demonstrated in *History of the Peloponnesian War* that the state's self-interested search for power or the need to balance against it was the true cause of a war (see Alker 1988). Machiavelli supported the idea that the ability to carry out an action (i.e. power) is a more important determinant of events than ethics or ideology (see Adams 1977, Lukes 2001). Hobbes argued that human beings' desire for power in the anarchic state of nature inevitably leads to wars unless the conflicting parties could establish a social contract (Hobbes 1994).[1]

---

[1]   However, recent interpretations regarding Machiavelli and Hobbes's perspective of power are more nuanced. For example, some authors suggest that Hobbes's notion of international anarchy refers to the anarchy of pre-political societies outside the ordered system of European states, instead of that of interstate relations later posited by realism (Moloney 2011).

To date, power continues to play a central role in the theoretical construction of realism. Classical realists such as Schuman and Morgenthau argue that all politics is a struggle for power (Morgenthau 1954, 25; Schuman 1933, 491). They view the world in a chaotic fashion without overriding authorities among all nations; that is why sovereign states are compelled to seek power to ensure their survival.

Morgenthau's definition of power has psychological underpinnings. He defines (political) power as 'a psychological relation between those who exercise it and those over whom it is exercised (Morgenthau 1954, 27).' Meanwhile, Morgenthau suggests that power can be generated from material (e.g., geography, natural resources, industrial capacity, military force, and population) and non-material resources (e.g., national character, moral, government, and diplomacy), although military power is considered as the most important means to carry out power. In his categorisation of power as military power, economic power, and power over opinion, Carr (1964, 109) makes it clear that 'the supreme importance of the military instrument lies in the fact that the *ultima ratio* of power in international relations is war.' Gilpin (1981, 13), who perceives power to be the military, economic, and technological capabilities of states, supports such a belief. Given its importance to the survival of a state, military power is not only used as a means, but also embraced as an end.

Prioritising military force in the conception of power offers several advantages for classical realism. Theoretically, it justifies the argument according to which military force can best serve as the means for states to secure their survival and dominance in an anarchic world. Unlike other methods, the use of military power almost ensures immediate effect (regardless of the outcome). It is the most salient mediator to demonstrate a state's power. Methodologically, it becomes possible to measure power by calculating a state's military capacities in a reductionist fashion. It also serves as a reference in realists' attempts to identify the issue of polarity and balancing in international politics.

If both *classical* and *structural* realists share the view that international politics is a continuous struggle for power, the two camps show divides when it comes to the driving force behind this struggle. For the latter, it is the anarchic system in international relations, and not human instinct, which prompts states to pursue power in order to ensure their security (Waltz 1989, 43).

Waltz views power as a property and rejects it to be relational. He is convinced that power can be generated by national attributes such as the size of population, territory, resource endowment, economic capability, military strength, political stability and competence (Waltz 1979, 131). These criteria enable Waltz to rank the overall capabilities of states and display the distribution of power in the international system. Despite his resistance against a relation-oriented power definition, he proposes that 'an agent is powerful to the extent that he affects others more than they affect him' – a notion close to Deutsch's (1953) relational power approach (Baldwin 2013, 285). Structural realists, like their classical counterparts, also privilege military force in their conception of power. Waltz argues that 'in international politics [military] force serves not only as the *ultimate ratio*, but also as the first and constant one (Waltz 1979, 113).' States' differences in military forces and other secondary elements result in a relative distribution of capabilities in the international system, which is the major independent variable explaining dependent variables such as wars, alliances, and the balance of power (Schmidt 2007, 54). As a result, power is a means to the end of security (Waltz 1989, 40).

The above view divides structural realists into two branches: 'defensive realism' because it perceives states to be 'security maximising-oriented' and as only seeking sufficient power to maintain this security; and secondly, 'offensive realism' because it sees states to be 'power maximising-oriented' in order to assure their survival in an anarchic international system. The latter branch goes so far to claim that all great powers have revisionist aims and pursue expansionist policies (see Mearsheimer 2001). Consequently, offensive realists embrace military power even more (e.g. the size and strength of the army) than their defensive counterparts do.

Several variants of realism maintain the assumption that the struggle for power and the anarchic world are states' motives for pursuing power, but they are on different level of analysis and independent variables when explaining international outcomes such as wars. Neoclassical realists, for instance, argue that the analysis of states' behaviours (mainly foreign policy) should take into account both domestic and structural levels (Walt 2002). Hence, Schweller believes that 'complex domestic political processes act as transmission belts that channel, mediate, and (re)direct policy outputs in response to external forces (i.e. changes in relative power) (2004, 164).'

Neoclassical realists also insist that military force is the major constituent of power. However, unlike their classical and structural counterparts, neo-classical realists claim that it is decision-makers' perception of power – rather than power itself - that matters in international politics (Wohlforth 1993, 2; Rose 1998, 147). Neoclassical realists moreover elaborate on the notion of 'state power' in reference to the ability of the government apparatus to 'extract national power for its ends (Zakaria 1998, 38-9).' Neoclassical realists inherit the idea from classical realism that a nation defines its interest in accordance to its power. That is, when the overall capability of a state increases, the state will pursue greater power in order to control the external environment, and vice versa. The struggle for power, to the neoclassical realists, is one important means permitting states to influence and control their living and external environment. In this sense, states are more 'influence-maximising oriented' than 'power-maximising oriented' or 'security-maximising oriented' (Zakaria 1998).

Overall, the realist conception of power demonstrates two characteristics. First, power is equivalent to military force. If realists acknowledge other sources of power, such as economic influence and technology, these sources are only of secondary importance. Second, power is property-oriented. That is, realists are solely interested in tangible, measurable materials as resources of power; they ignore the relational aspect of power (i.e. how A exercises power over B in order to make B comply to his wishes).

The Midlife Crisis of Power in Realism[2]

Several scholars (Baldwin 2013; Schmidt 2007; Grieco 2007) have pointed out severe deficiencies in realism's conception of power, which results in the debate about the worthy existence of realism as a theory. While some evoke the death of realism (Kapstein 1995, 149), I would suggest that realism is experiencing a midlife crisis. This view is related to realism's incomplete achievement and the decreasing importance of military power.

The contemporary literature exposes that realists tend to overemphasise the importance of military force for states' survival in the anarchic international system to the extent that military might – also referred as 'hard power' – is taken as the superior means in states' struggle for power.[3] To realists, a country can best defend itself and assure its national security by equipping itself with a large arsenal of weapons, nuclear missiles, a large army, naval

---

[2] The term 'midlife crisis,' first coined by the psychologist Elliot Jaques in 1965, is employed here in a metaphoric fashion to depict the struggling state and the dysfunction of power in realism. After all, midlife crisis 'commonly involves reflection on what the individual has done with his or her life up to that point, often with feelings that not enough has been accomplished (Mendez 2008, 565; see also Edwards and Byrd 2008).'

[3] Some scholars disagree that hard power equates to military force because hard power is mostly a contrary concept of soft power. For the concept of soft power and its comparison to hard power, see Nye (1990; 2004; 2011). They also suggest that military force is only one form of power. However, given the supreme role of military force in realism's conception of power, I use hard power and military force in an interchangeable fashion.

and air forces, etc. Some branches of realism value military force as the only means in a country's offensive policies.

However, this over-emphasis of hard power prompts realism to march into theoretic and empirical dead ends for three reasons. First, realism fails to see the difference between potential power and actual power. That is, having important military assets does not guarantee their transformation into real power. The most obvious example is the nuclear weapons which owner countries are potentially unable to use in conflict due to their disastrous consequences. Second, a large variation of wars (e.g. conventional, biological, civil, asymmetric, cyber, etc.) renders tangible military resources to be ineffective from one case to another. In a cyber-war, the enemy might paralyze the whole infrastructure of a country simply by hacking into the government's central information system. Likewise, militarily poor-equipped terrorist groups can use civil aviation, vehicle, or human bombs as weapons to strike a super-power in an asymmetric war. Third, possessing hard power is perhaps crucial in warfare, but winning a war does not ensure success if one takes the issue of costs and benefits into account (Knorr 1966). For instance, even though the Bush administration overthrew the regime of Saddam Hussein in 2003, the triumph was eclipsed by the US's colossal spending of money and materials as well as its failure to restore peace in the region in the aftermath of the war (Stiglitz and Bilmes, 2008).

Today's states do not abandon hard power, but they no longer prioritise it as they did before. Since the end of Cold War, major powers in the West have tended to limit their military expenditure to less than 3% of their GDP.[4] There is a prevailing belief that building mutual trust is more effective to retain peace than engaging in armament competition that leads to security dilemma. Moreover, imposing economic sanctions—and not resorting to military forces—stands as a frequent measure for major powers to deal with international conflicts. Such a tendency can be observed in the international community's reaction regarding North Korea's continuous development of its nuclear arsenal in 2013 and 2016, or to Russia's invasion of Ukraine/Crimea in 2014.

The shrinking importance of hard power is not only caused by its incompatibility with a peaceful world, but also because it is being overshadowed by the growing popularity of soft power. Soft power gains its analytical purchase at the expense of the losing utility of hard power (Schmidt 2007, 62). Today, major powers, rising powers, or regional powers are more concerned about how to cultivate their general capacities and expand influences worldwide without conveying an offensive image in the world; this

---

[4]   See SIPRI Military Expenditure Database, https://www.sipri.org/databases/milex

is where soft power can better justify its existence and legitimacy than hard power. Soft power, a term coined by Joseph Nye, is a concept inspired by Bachrach and Baratz's (1962; 1963) 'second face of power.' Nye (1990, 31) sees soft power as 'an indirect way to exercise power other than resting on inducements (carrots) or threats (sticks).' He defines soft power to be 'getting others to want what you want' and explains that 'co-optive [soft] power can rest on the attraction of one's ideas or on the ability to set the political agenda in a way that shapes the preferences that others express.' For the difference between soft power and hard power, Nye argues that

> The distinction is one of degree, both in the nature of the behavior and in the tangibility of the resources. Both types are aspects of the ability to achieve one's purposes by controlling the behavior of others. Command power [hard power]—the ability to change what others do—can rest on coercion or inducement. Co-optive power [soft power]—the ability to shape what others want—can rest on the attractiveness of one's culture and ideology or the ability to manipulate the agenda of political choices in a manner that makes actors fail to express some preferences because they seem to be too unrealistic (Nye 1990, 267).

Governments now are more willing to develop their soft power by designing relevant policy tools such as establishing overseas cultural institutes, propagating ideology through global broadcasting services, exporting higher education, promoting tourism, etc. Soft power has also become one of the major indexes when analysts attempt to measure a state's general capacity (Treverton and Seth 2005). In a sense, the struggle for power today has a new meaning: to use soft power to attract more allies is a better approach to secure a state's survival than to use hard power to annihilate enemies.

Power, Realism and the Rise of China

Realism's power concept becomes problematic when applied to the case of China. If classical realism's balance of power found its empirical ground in Europe, notably in early 19th century, this is not the case in the East. Imperial China had been the region's only superpower over centuries and its neighbour states rarely contested such hegemony. This long-lasting unipolar system also contradicts the argument of structural realism of which a bipolar system is the key to stability in an anarchic international system. From 3 BCE to the 19th century, the Chinese dynasty was able to maintain its central position in the tributary system, surrounded by 'uncivilised' neighbours such as Mongolia, Xinjiang, Tibet, Korea, Annam (present-day Vietnam), Siam

(Thailand), Burma (Myanmar), and Nepal (Cohen 2000; Wills 2010).

The Chinese perception of war is irrelevant to realism as military force is not considered *ultimate ratio*. From the prevalence of 'The Art of War,' authored by the renowned strategist Sun Tzu, imperial China put greater importance on a well-considered logistics system and strategic visions to prevent a war rather than on strengthening military forces to strike a war. China's use of force was commonly not exercised for the purpose of self-defence, as realism stipulates. More frequently, it has moral underpinnings. For example, the breakout of the first Sino-Japanese War in 1894 was derived from the attempt of the Chinese Qing dynasty to protect Korea against Japan's invasion. What contradicts realism is that, despite its military inferiority vis-à-vis the empire of Japan - after its successful Meiji Restoration – the Qing dynasty still decided to go to war against Japan (Shih 1993, 134-6).

Even today, China continues to go astray from the power trajectory posited by realism. Looking back at its historical account of wars, the People's Republic of China (PRC) can hardly be qualified as a 'rational actor' in the way realism understands the term. The Sino-Vietnamese War in 1979 well illustrates China's uncommon behaviours in world politics. The war, also surnamed as 'The Punishing War,' was driven by China's intention to punish Vietnam for attacking its protégé, the communist Cambodia of Pol Pot, and for siding with the Soviet Union. In the war, the Chinese People's Liberation Army (PLA) dominated the Viet Cong army and seized several important sites in both North and South Vietnam within a month. Once it had declared victory, however, China surprisingly withdrew itself from the occupied regions. Similar patterns can be discerned in the Sino-Indian War in 1962 and China's quasi war over Zhenbao Island against the Soviet Union in 1969 (Shih 1993).

China's authoritarian regime and growing overall capabilities prompt many realist scholars to believe that a war is inevitable between China and the current superpower or even regional powers (e.g. Japan, India). According to this logic, China's fast rising in the world should jeopardise American hegemony. China is often perceived to be a bigger threat than the US by the international community. To the supporters of democracy, a superpower led by a communist regime is simply unimaginable. A violent debate over the 'China threat' was ignited in 1995 when Charles Krauthammer, an American journalist, published an essay, depicting China as a 'bully (...) as it tries relentlessly to expand its reach,' and exhorted that the US should contain China (Roy 1996, 759). The offensive realist John Mearsheimer (2001) even went far to suggest that China's emerging power and influence must be contained by any means.

Nevertheless, China's conduct in world politics so far does not allow realists to qualify it as a 'revisionist state'[5] who, following their logic, should always have been seeking to overturn the American hegemony; nor does the rising of China result in instability in East Asia or beyond. Overall, the rising of China does not affect the stability of the current unipolar international system. The 'China threat' evaluated by much of the realist analyses is mainly grounded on China's building-up of hard power. However, in recent years, China's enthusiasm for developing soft power programs implies that hard power is no longer the sole priority in Chinese foreign policy.

Since 2003, China has been undertaking even more efforts on developing its soft power in order to shape an image of peaceful rising. In 2014, the annual report made public by the Chinese People's Political Consultative Conference (CPPCC) explained that the PRC's military expenditure only occupied 1.4% of the country's GNP (gross national product).[6] Meanwhile, China has been developing tools to increase its soft power in the world. These efforts include support for infrastructure-related projects in Africa and Latin America, the creation of the Confucius Institutes for promoting the Chinese language and culture worldwide, media such as the CCTV and China Radio International to broadcast about the 'good' China, and the hosting of important international events such as Olympic Games or World Exhibitions to increase international exposure. Comparing to the past, contemporary China is also more inclined to conform to international norms on issue areas like free trade, nuclear non-proliferation and environmental protection.

Overall, the rise of China does not follow the scenario of realism, for two reasons. First, military forces are not the most important means to exercise power for China. Soft power comes as an important strategy in China's recent foreign policy-making. In addition, China's use of military force can be somehow irrational, as we have observed from its historical track. Second, China does not act like a 'revisionist state.' It does not strive to change the current balance of power; nor is it keen on immediately becoming the next superpower by engaging in war with the US.

---

[5]   Structural realist uses the term 'revisionist state' to portray a state's intention to use forces in order to alter the balance of power. It opposes to a 'status-quo state' who prefers to maintain the current balance.

[6]   See http://news.xinhuanet.com/english/special/2014-03/05/c_133161044.htm (accessed 20 June 2016). However, many countries, international organisations, and think tanks contest the transparency of this report and believe that the PRC's military budget already reached 2.3% of its GNP in 2003 and grows at a rate of 7% to 10% annually, although such rate is still far behind that of the United States. See http://www.globalsecurity.org/military/world/china/budget.htm (accessed 20 June 2016)

After the Midlife Crisis

A review of the literature exposes that realism's major conception of power, which casts a heavy focus on hard power, is problematic. Its theoretic construct seems to be over-simplified and is unable to explain and predict many international outcomes. As is explained in the previous section, neither classical realism, nor its structural and neorealist counterparts have rightly explained or foreseen the past or recent development of China in world politics. For, the realist tends to regard China as the next superpower who will challenge the American hegemony and destabilise the current unipolar system. Nevertheless, the belief of a 'China threat' can be merely an imaginary fear built on the assumption that China's hard power would endanger western civilisation. Until today, there is no (or not yet) clear evidence showing that China manifests revisionist tendencies.

Can realism cope with the struggle of achievement and solve the midlife crisis? Despite significant amendments of several 'neo' schools, realism still suffers from empirical inconsistency. The reason is straightforward – its fundamental principles of power never change: neo-classical realists still favour the concept of the balance of power when explaining international conflicts, structural realists still believe in a bipolar international system headed by the US and China in the future, and offensive realists never give up the superior means of hard power in world politics. Consequently, there is no room for optimism regarding the future of realism. Kapstein (1995) acknowledges that the dissidents of realism point out several fatal flaws of the theory, but he also argues that the theory cannot be overthrown as long as there is no better theory to replace it thoroughly. However, such an argument is irrelevant. For the very existence of a theory depends on its ability to explain and to predict the occurrence of a phenomenon, and not on the existence (or not) of another (dominant) theory. A problematic theory will eventually lose its attraction in front of its public with or without the emergence of a better theory. If realism is unable to readjust its conception of power by theoretically taking into account the equal importance of other faces of power and by empirically looking at the international outcomes beyond the Western sphere, it will be difficult to expect a rejuvenation after the midlife crisis.

References

Adams, Robert M. 1977. *Niccolo Machiavelli, The Prince: A New Translation, Backgrounds, Interpretations, Peripherica*. New York: Norton & Co.

Alker, Hayward R. Jr. 1988. "The Dialectical Logic of Thucydides' Melian Dialogue". *The American Political Science Review*, 82(3): 805–820.

Bachrach, Peter and Morton S. Baratz. 1962. "Two Faces of Power". *American Political Science Review* 56(4): 947–952.

Bachrach, Peter and Morton S. Baratz. 1963. "Decisions and Nondecisions: An Analytical Framework". *American Political Science Review* 57(3): 632–42.

Baldwin, David A. 2013. "Power and International Relations". *Handbook of International Relations*, edited by Walter Carlsnaes, Thomas Risse and Beth A. Simmons, 273–297. London: Sage Publications.

Carr, Edward H. 1964. *The Twenty Years' Crisis: 1919–1939*. New York: Harper & Row.

Cohen, Warren I. 2000. *East Asia at the Center: Four Thousand Years of Engagement with the World*. New York: Columbia University Press.

Deutsch, Karl W. 1953. *Nationalism and Social Communication*. Cambridge, MA: MIT Press.

Edwards, Christopher L. and Goldie Byrd. 2008. "Midlife Crisis." *International Encyclopedia of the Social Sciences*, edited by William A. Jr, 148–151. Detroit: Macmillan Reference USA.

Gilpin, Robert. 1981. *War and Change in World Politics*. New York: Cambridge University Press.

Grieco, Joseph M. 2007. "Structural Realism and the Problem of Polarity and War". *Power in World Politics*, edited by F. Berenskoetter and M. J Williams, 64–82. New York: Routledge.

Hobbes, Thomas. 1994. *Leviathan*. Edited by Edwin Curley. Indianapolis: Hackett.

Kapstein, Ethan B. 1995. "Is Realism Dead? The Domestic Sources of International Politics". *International Organization* 49(4):751–774.

Knorr, Klaus. 1966. *On the Uses of Military Power in the Nuclear Age*. New Jersey: Princeton University Press.

Lukes, Timothy J. 2001. "Lionizing Machiavelli". *The American Political Science Review* 95(3): 561–575.

Mearsheimer, John J. 2001. *The Tragedy of Great Power Politics*. New York: W. W. Norton.

Mendez, Nancy. 2008. "Midlife crisis". *Encyclopedia of Aging and Public Health*, edited by JD Loue Sana and Martha Sajatovic, 565–6. New York: Springer US.

Moloney, Pat 2011. "Hobbes, Savagery, and International Anarchy". *American Political Science Review* 105(1): 189–204.

Morgenthau, Hans J. 1954. *Politics among Nations: The Struggle for Power and Peace*. 2nd ed. Chicago, IL: University of Chicago Press.

Nye, Joseph. 1990. *Bound to Lead*. New York: Basic Books.

Nye, Joseph. 2004. *Soft Power: The Means to Success in World Politics*. New York: Public Affairs.

Nye, Joseph. 2011. *The Future of Power*. New York: Public Affairs.

Rose, Gideon. 1998. "Neoclassical Realism and Theories of Foreign Policy". *World Politics* 51(1): 144–172.

Roy, Denny. 1996. "The 'China Threat' Issue: Major Arguments". *Asian Survey* 36(8): 758–771.

Schmidt, Brian. 2007. "Realist Conceptions of Power". *Power in World Politics*, edited by Felix Berenskoetter and M. J. Williams, 43–63. New York: Routledge.

Schuman, Frederick L. 1933. *International Politics: An Introduction to the Study of the Western State System*. New York: McGraw Hill.

Schweller, Randall L. 2004. "Unanswered Threats: A Neoclassical Realist Theory of Under-balancing". *International Security* 29(2): 159–201.

Shih, Chih-Yu. 1993. *China's Just World: The Morality of Chinese Foreign Policy*. Colorado: Lynne Rienner Publisher.

Stiglitz, Joseph E. and Linda Bilmes. 2008. *The Three Trillion Dollar War: The True Cost of the Iraq Conflict*. New York: Norton.

Treverton, Gregory F. and Jones G. Seth. 2005. *Measuring National Power*. Santa Barbara, CA: RAND Corporation.

Walt, Stephen M. 2002. "The Enduring Relevance of the Realist Tradition". *Political Science. The State of the Discipline*, edited by I. Katznelson and H. V. Milner, 197–230. New York: Norton.

Waltz, Kenneth N. 1979. *Theory of International Politics*. London: Addison Wesley.

Waltz, Kenneth N. 1989. "The Origins of War in Neorealist Theory". *The Origin and Prevention of Major Wars*, edited by R. Rotberg and T. K. Rabb, 39–52. Cambridge: Cambridge University Press.

Wills, John E. 2010. *Past and Present in China's Foreign Policy: From 'Tribute System' to 'Peaceful Rise'*. Portland, ME: Merwin Asia.

Wohlforth, William C. 1993. *The Elusive Balance*. Ithaca, NY: Cornell University Press.

Zakaria, Fareed. 1998. *From Wealth to Power*. Princeton, NJ: Princeton University Press.

5

Realism and Power Transition Theory: Different Branches of the Power Tree

CARSTEN RAUCH

After the end of the Cold War, realism or, to be more precise, almost all power based approaches to International Relations, have been largely written off by scholars for their failure to predict the conflict's ending, as well as for their inability to deal with the phenomena that became most relevant for IR in the decades that followed, for example norms, ideas, the impact of regime types and so on.

However, the comeback of great power conflicts and the blatancy of global power shifts has led to a kind of resurgence of theoretical approaches that focus on the role of power. In Syria and Ukraine the US and Russia are supporting different sides, and Cold War frontlines seem to re-emerge. Considering the fate of Ukraine (a country that voluntarily gave up its nuclear weapons after the Cold War for security assurances by the great powers including Russia), some scholars have even begun to wonder whether realists who praised nuclear deterrence (and thus warned countries that had already acquired nuclear weapons not to give them up) were not right after all. And considering the meteoric rise of China, scholars are increasingly beginning to utilise the theoretical lens of power transition theory (PTT) to evaluate its potential impact on international security (Lee 2015; Kim and Gates 2015; Lim 2014; Jeffery 2009; Levy 2008; Lemke and Tammen 2006).

But even though both, realism and PTT, emphasise the influence of international power constellations, it makes a stark difference which of the two approaches one uses for assessing the international situation. While both are often merged together (mostly by scholars who subscribe to neither), it is important to regard and embrace them as different branches of the power tree that, most of the time and despite some common roots, lead to quite different analyses and policy prescriptions.

In the following article I will first describe what I understand as (balance-of-power) realism and power transition theory. I will then trace their conceptual differences and show under what conditions they lead to the same (less often) or differing (more often) conclusions. Finally, I show how the rise of China calls for quite different policies depending on the theoretical choice between realism and PTT.

Realism, Power Transition Theory and their Major Differences

Realism and power transition theory are both well-known approaches to the study of international politics, so it might suffice to summarise them in a nutshell here. Realism can be traced back to thinkers like Machiavelli and Hobbes. Modern proponents include scholars like Hans Joachim Morgenthau (1954), Kenneth Waltz (1979) and John J. Mearsheimer (2001), among many others. After classical realism had put much emphasis on human nature and the *animus dominandi*, more recent versions have rather focused on the structure of the international system (anarchy), the functionality of the units (same) and the distribution of capabilities. Waltz famously explained that only two requirements are necessary for his theory to work: 'that the order be anarchic and that it be populated by units wishing to survive' (Waltz 1979, 121). Whenever these conditions are met, Waltz maintained, balance-of-power politics prevail. Balance-of-power theory in turn can be summarised as arguing 'that changes in the distribution of power are often dangerous' (Lobell 2016, 33).

Power transition theory was originally brought forward by A. F. K. Organski (1958) and has been further developed by Organski, Jacek Kugler and a number of other scholars. Its central claims are that the international system is usually hierarchically ordered with a dominant power at the top that creates and sustains the international order; that, because of uneven growth rates, new powers are regularly rising; and that the risk of war is highest in a situation when a dissatisfied rising power has reached parity or even overtaken the declining dominant power (Lemke 2004, 55–6).

Both (balance-of-power) realism and power transition theory are concerned with war and peace in the international system, focus on the state as the central actor and put a special emphasis on the role of power. Because of these similarities, PTT is often regarded as a variant or branch of realism. Some scholars go as far as to blend both approaches in a kind of imaginary 'realist power transition theory' (see for example Silvius 2014; Khoo 2013; He and Feng 2013; Herrington 2011; Changhe 2008; Christensen 2001). On the following pages I challenge this view and highlight the differences between realism (more specifically balance-of-power realism) and power transition theory.

Despite the obvious fact that realism's perspective on international politics and the distribution of power is rather cross-sectional (looking at a certain point in time), while PTT's perspective is rather longitudinal (looking at a development over time), and the ontological disagreement whether the international system usually resembles more anarchy (realism) or a hierarchy (PTT), there are two major differences that I want to discuss below: the meaning of different power constellations and the relevance of the sub-systemic factor of satisfaction with the status quo. Taking these differences seriously, I argue, leads to widely differing policy prescriptions depending on which perspective one employs.

Same Constellations, Different Analysis

The first central difference that I want to highlight in this article concerns the question of how a system should be configured to achieve the highest possible stability and peacefulness. All kinds of realism are united in that they believe that a harmony of interests between the differing powers in the international system is only an illusion and that interests are rather colliding constantly. In order to ensure peace among these conflicting interests, a stable balance of power is necessary. 'From the perspective of balance-of-power theorists, the power preponderance of a single state or of a coalition of states is highly undesirable because the preponderant actor is likely to engage in aggressive behavior' (Paul 2004, 5). When this balance of power is disturbed or when one power strives to (and succeeds in) enhancing its power position disproportionately, war becomes likely (Lobell 2016, 33). Thus, those who want to preserve peace would be wise to organise their foreign policy (and choice of alliance partners) in a way that preserves or restores the balance of power in the international system.

PTT pioneers have always questioned this reasoning and understood themselves as antipodes instead of proponents of such a view. This becomes especially apparent when PTT authors ponder how the international system should be configured in order to minimise the probability of (great power) war. Proponents of PTT believe that an equilibrium of power (at least between the top two competitors) is indeed not a guarantee of peace but quite the opposite: an invitation to war (Siverson and Miller 1996, 58). A system, according to PTT, is more peaceful when there is no balance but a large imbalance and the most powerful state is predominant. Only in such a case is the result of an armed conflict clearly foreseeable and it thus does not make sense for either side to risk it. 'A preponderance of power on the one side [...] increases the chances of peace, for the greatly stronger side need not fight at all to get what it wants, while the weaker side would be plainly foolish to attempt to battle for what it wants' (Organski 1968, 294–5). In cases where predominance is not established and either side can conceivably hope for victory (or at least for preventing defeat), war is a much more attractive option. Therefore, a main difference between balance-of-power realism and PTT is, as Tammen and Kugler put it: 'Under balance of power, relative power equilibrium insures the peace. Under power parity or power transition, relative power equilibrium increases the probability of war' (Tammen and Kugler 2006, 40, Footnote 6).

However, when proponents of PTT criticise balance-of-power realism they often use an understanding of *balance* that is more akin to their own theoretical concept of *parity* (see for example Lemke and Kugler 1996, 5ff). It thus appears necessary to define the differences between the concepts of balance and parity.

Parity – in the sense of PTT – means that in a dyad or group of states all participating states have a comparable amount of power (usually +/- 20% constitutes the corridor of parity, that is a power A with 100 units of power is in parity with all other powers that have between 80 and 120 units of power). The (political) relations between these powers are not relevant. A balance, on the other hand, is in effect in the international (or a regional) system when there is equilibrium between the most important alliances taken together, while the power-relation between single protagonists might be subject to grave disparities. Figure 1 illustrates this with different models or ideal-types of power constellations.

Figure 1: Balance and Parity in Different Constellations

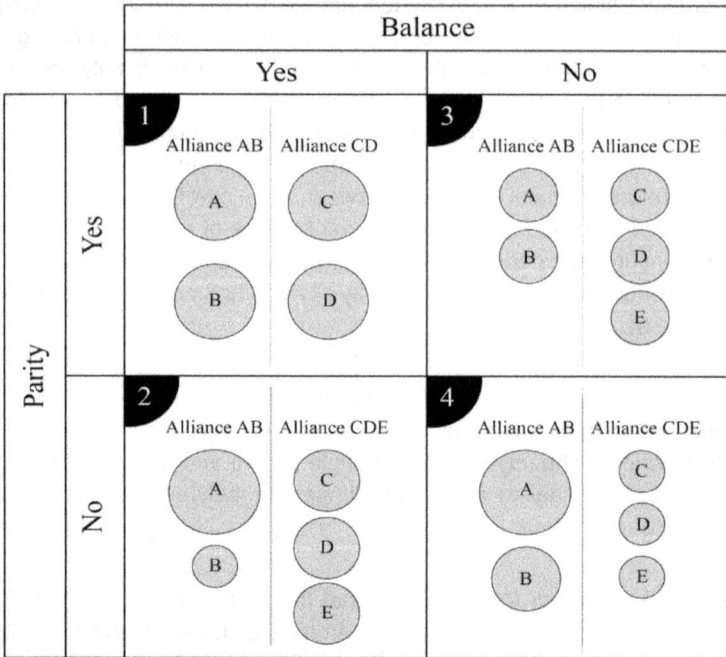

Model 1 in the upper left shows four great powers with a similar amount of power. As all great powers are in the 80% corridor of the dominant power, there is a situation of parity between them. As they are also organised in two opposing alliances of equal strength we can also say that the system is balanced. Model 2 in the lower left shows a system with five great powers. There is one power (state A) that is clearly predominant. No other state reaches at least 80% of its power capacity; thus there is no parity. At the same time, A is allied with the weakest power (state B) so that the combined capacity of their alliance equals that of the alliance made up of C, D and E. The system is thus in balance.

In Model 3 in the upper right we have five powers again, but this time of equal strength, thus creating a five-way parity. However, as the alliance of A and B is much weaker than the alliance of C, D and E, the system is in imbalance. Finally, Model 4 in the lower right shows a system where there is neither balance, nor parity. Among the five great powers in the system, state A is clearly predominant. This mirrors Model 2. However, differing from Model 2, the two alliances in this system are not balanced. A is not allied with the weakest power (as in model 2) but with the second strongest power (state B). The alliance of A and B is thus much more powerful than the opposing alliance of C, D and E; the system is therefore in imbalance.

The four models in Figure 1 thus show different possibilities for relating parity and balance to each other under different configurations of power and alliances. As we can see, there are configurations that can be seen as both (Model 1) or neither (Model 4) in balance and/or in parity. Models 2 and 3 furthermore show that there are situations possible in which a power configuration is in balance, but not parity – or vice versa. Depending on which concept (and underlying theoretical reasoning) one uses, differing valuations of these configurations become possible. If we do not properly differentiate between the two concepts, proponents of PTT, for example, might accuse realists of certifying Model 3 a relatively high peacefulness, given the distribution of power among the five actors shows a situation of parity. However, Model 3 might show parity but still no real balance of power as the alliance CDE is clearly stronger than alliance AB.

Ceteris paribus – and in a simplified way – realism and PTT agree on the relative peacefulness of these models in two of the four cases, that is when parity and balance do *not* concur (Model 2 and 3). In Model 2 with no parity but balance both would suggest that the system will likely be rather peaceful; in Model 3 with no balance but parity both would suggest that conflict is likely. Regarding the other two models, however, realism and PTT come to contrary conclusions. In Model 1 where we can speak of both parity and balance, PTT expects conflict between the dominant power and at least one of the other powers in parity, while realism expects peace through a stable balance of power. In Model 4 where we have neither parity nor balance, PTT expects the preponderance to foster peace, while realism fears that the imbalance might lead to conflict.

The (Un-)Importance of Satisfaction with the Status Quo

The second central difference between the theories that I want to discuss here relates to the fact that realism is notorious for treating the state as a unitary actor and, even more, a black box. States are essentially the same and only differ because of their different placement in the international system and their different amount of capabilities (Frankel 1996, 321; Waltz 2008). While it is true that classical realists have worked with concepts like revolutionary and status quo powers (Aron 1966; Wolfers 1962; Kissinger 1957) and some modern realists have striven to 'bring the revisionist state back in' (Schweller 1994; also see Rynning and Ringsmose 2008), revisionism and dissatisfaction remain out of the purview of balance-of-power logic. According to this logic, it is not the properties of any given state that decides how it behaves internationally but rather the existing distribution of power or, maybe, the distribution of threat (Walt 1987).

Power transition theory, on the other hand, depends on the unit level variable of satisfaction with the status quo which – in order for the theory to prevent becoming self-referential – cannot be dependent on the state's placement in the international order a.k.a. its amount of capabilities (Rauch 2014, 209–15). It belongs to the core of PTT that rising powers are often (but not always) dissatisfied with the international order, an order that – according to PTT – has been created by the dominant power (Lemke 2004, 56–7). This dissatisfaction stems from the fact that the order in many ways benefits its creator along with its allies, while rising powers are being disadvantaged or at least perceive themselves so (Tammen et al. 2000, 9). For this reason, dissatisfied rising powers become challengers to the international order, striving at least to reform and at most to shatter the existing order and to build a new one. The dominant power, on the other hand, is not inclined to give up 'its' international order voluntarily. In order to establish a new order, the rising power thus has to resort to the use of force (Rauch 2014, 49–52). This is why great power war happens according to PTT. Peaceful power transitions, on the other hand, are possible if the rising power is satisfied with the status quo (Kim and Gates 2015, 220; Paul and Shankar 2014; Tammen et al. 2000, 26). The power constellation thus only tells us half of the story according to PTT. It is the combination of opportunity and motivation, of a parity-situation and dissatisfaction that constitutes a danger for the stability of the international order (Nolte 2010, 888; Lemke 2004, 57). (Dis-)Satisfaction is thus a variable. Realists, on the other hand, often regard dissatisfaction – if they consider it as all – as an analytical constant. Mearsheimer (2001, 35), for example, posits that 'states do not become status quo powers until they completely dominate the system', thereby rendering *all* non-dominant great powers necessarily dissatisfied. And even if state preferences are not regarded as fixed, the logic of the security dilemma demands to always assume the worst from your neighbours as non-aggressive intentions might a) change quickly and b) might diminish one's own security (even if unintentionally).

To sum up: The most important differences (among some others) between balance of power realism and power transition theory concern a) the different meaning of balance and parity, which leads to differing evaluations concerning the conflict-proneness of the same power constellation in two out of four ideal types; and b) the different significance both approaches ascribe to the factor of satisfaction with the status quo of the international order.

The Rise of China: Balance it? Embrace it? Manage it?

What do these differences imply for the analysis and interpretation of global power shifts in general and the emergence and rise of powers like China and India in particular? Utilising gross domestic product as a crude power indicator we can describe the current global power constellation as follows.

If we take nominal GDP ratings as indicator for state power, as of 2015 the United States is still in a leading position globally. Its GDP of 17,946,996 million current US Dollars is only slightly lower than that of the following three powers (China, Japan and Germany) combined. Additionally, two of these three powers (Japan and Germany) are allied with the US. Even if we look at the rest of the top ten-ranked countries according to GDP, we find a number of powers allied or on good terms with the United States (France, United Kingdom, Italy and India), no committed ally of China and two powers whose allegiance is as of yet unclear (Brazil and Russia). An imbalance of power thus exists and it favours Washington.

Turning to power developments we see, however, that this might change. According to GDP growth rates, the United States was in decline in relation to China (growing more slowly) in all years between 1990 and 2013, in decline in relation to India in all but two years (1997 and 2000), in decline in relation to Brazil for 15 years, and in decline in relation to Russia for 13 years and in all but one year since 1999 (see Figure 2).

Figure 2: GDP growth trends of the Top 10 Powers according to nominal GDP in 2013 over time (in constant 2012 billion US$)

	1990-2013	1990-1999	2000-2009	2010-2013
United States	2.47	3.24	1.82	2.17
China	9.92	10.00	10.29	8.77
Japan	1.16	1.47	0.56	1.89
Germany	1.60	2.20	0.83	2.04
France	1.62	2.01	1.42	1.17
United Kingdom	1.92	2.08	1.94	1.49
Brazil	2.66	1.70	3.32	3.45
Italy	0.76	1.48	0.54	-0.47
Russia	0.80	-4.91	5.48	3.38
India	6.39	5.77	6.90	6.66

The rise of China in particular (but also India and to a lesser extent Brazil) becomes even more pronounced when these growth rates are projected into the future. Taken together, the BRICS (Brazil, India, Russia, China, South Africa) will – according to a UNDP report – surpass the combined GDP of the Europe and the United States by 2020 (Lobell 2016, 34). China alone will – according to Goldman Sachs – match the United States GDP by the end of the 2020s (O'Neill and Stupnytska 2009, 24). The BRICS, however, are not a stable alliance that would support China under all circumstances (Nossel 2016, van Agtmael 2012, Bosco 2011). While Moscow might lean closer to Beijing given its conflicts with Washington (Sputnik News 2016), New Delhi has in the recent years rather strengthened its ties to the United States (Müller and Schmidt 2009, Rauch 2008). The US itself, on the other hand, has – as has been pointed out above – a number of powerful allies in all parts of the world, from other NATO members up to Japan and Australia. Let us try to situate the current and expected future power constellations within the typology introduced above: The current situation (US still much more powerful than China, US alliance much more powerful than China and its friends) might resemble most closely model 4 (no balance, no parity). If the rise of China goes on as expected this might change into a situation that rather resembles Model 2 (no balance but parity).

Balance-of-power theory suggests that such a rise – as in fact any meaningful rise of power of any actor in the international system – might become problematic as it disturbs the current power configuration. This theory might furthermore suggest that the best reply to the rise of China and India could be to create strong alliances (or strengthen the existing ones) in order to build stable counterbalances. Maybe one of the rising powers (most likely India) can even be utilised to help balancing the other one (most likely China). However, looking at the snapshot of the current global power constellations, China still remains far removed from the leading position which is still held by the United States. Taking into account alliances, the imbalance (in favour of Washington) becomes even more pronounced. A different picture emerges only when one explicitly focuses on the Asian theatre where China's rise has already had a much larger impact. President Obama's Pivot to Asia (Liegl and Wolf 2016) might thus seem a sensible move in order to bring the region back into balance.

The outlook based on PTT is generally characterised by concerns, too. Looking not only at the present power constellation but also the underlying dynamics it would highlight that for at least two and a half decades China has been growing faster than the United States, and that these trends give reason to expect a continuing catching-up process of (at least) China. However, PTT would also suggest that conflict is most likely when China or India reach parity with the United States or with each other. As at least the former seems to be a little down the road (especially once the power of the US' allies is taken into consideration), one policy advice of PTT for the United States would be to ensure that this power gap does not close. Preponderance brings peace and parity is prone to war. Hence, Washington should do everything it can to prevent a peer competitor to emerge or, at a minimum, strengthen its own power position. On the other hand, PTT, while being alarmed by the impending conversion of the power trajectories of the dominant and the rising power, would also ask whether the rising powers are satisfied with the status quo of the international order. Herein lies the key to conflict and peace. If the rising powers are found to be extremely and irredeemably dissatisfied, then PTT proper would suggest counter measures in the same as does balance-of-power theory. If, however, the rising powers are found to be only slightly or not at all dissatisfied, PTT would counsel not to risk causing dissatisfaction by alienating the rising powers but rather to put measures in effect that mitigate dissatisfaction and make the rising powers share and stakeholders of the international order (Paul 2016; Rauch 2014, 275–80).

Unfortunately, not all PTT research and PTT-driven commentaries take the centrality of the satisfaction variable seriously. All too often one finds perspectives that I call *PTT light* camouflaging for PTT (Rauch 2014, 65–8). PTT light is characterised by its focus on power transitions (often even between great powers as such and not only at the top of the international order) and its careless to total neglect of satisfaction with the status quo. While this is a mere nuisance in academia (for example when 'PTT' is tested without including satisfaction in the research design) it can become dangerous when it transgresses into actual politics. Slogans like 'history teaches us that rising powers are likely to provoke war' (Shirk 2007, 4) or '[t]hroughout the history of the modern international state system, ascending powers have always challenged the position of the dominant (hegemonic) power in the international system – and these challenges have usually culminated in war' (Layne 2008, 16) may sound pronounced but have little in common with a sophisticated PTT perspective and risk turning into a self-fulfilling prophecy.

Conclusion

Though balance-of-power realism and power transition theory are related by their mutual focus on the distribution or development of power in the international system, I have argued that both are distinct and differing research agendas. For starters, they disagree about which power constellation is least war-prone. PTT suggests that the most peaceful international order is one with a power preponderance, while realism prefers a stable equilibrium of power. And even if their central concepts of *balance* and *parity* sound comparable, they should not be mixed up. There are constellations in which balance and parity fall together, yet there are likewise constellations in which a balance exists but no parity and vice versa. Thus, their joint focus on power does not lead balance-of-power realism and power transition theory to similar conclusions.

Applying this to the current power shifts and, most notably, the rise of China, I have argued that balance-of-power realism and power transition theory not only come to differing evaluations concerning the perilousness of the situation but also prescribe quite different policy choices to deal with the situation. This article is not about which of these perspectives is (analytically, empirically or normatively) more sound, but about highlighting that these differing perspectives exist and that it matters a great deal whether one regards current events through balance-of-power or power-transition glasses.

References

Aron, Raymond. 1966. *Peace and War: A Theory of International Relations*. Garden City, NJ: Doubleday.

Bosco, David. 2011. "Are the BRICs a Political Alliance". (http://foreignpolicy. com/2011/03/23/are-the-brics-a-political-alliance accessed October 16, 2016)

Changhe, Su. 2008. "The Role of the United States in Cross-Strait Negotiations: A Mainland Chinese Perspective" in *Conflict Management, Security and Intervention in East Asia: Third-party Mediation in Regional Conflict*, edited by Jacob Bercovitch, Kwei-Bo Huang, and Chung-Chian Teng, 217–31. London: Routledge.

Christensen, Thomas J. 2001. "Posing Problems without Catching Up: China's Rise and Challenges for U.S. Security Policy". *International Security* 25(4): 5–40.

DiCicco, Jonathan M. and Jack S. Levy. 2003. "The Power Transition Research Program – A Lakatosian Analysis" in *Progress in International Relations Theory: Appraising the Field*, edited by Colin Elman and Miriam Fendius Elman, 109–57. Cambridge, MA: MIT Press.

Finel, Bernard I. 2001/2002. "Black Box or Pandora's Box: State Level Variables and Progressivity in Realist Research Programs." *Security Studies* 11(2): 187–227.

Frankel, Benjamin. 1996. *Roots of Realism*. London, Portland, OR: Frank Cass.

Global Security Newswire. 2014. "Should Ukraine Have Gotten Rid of Its Cold War Nukes?". Accessed 30 May 2016. http://www.nti.org/gsn/article/should-ukraine-have-gotten-rid-its-nukes/

He, Kai, and Huiyun Feng. 2013. *Prospect Theory and Foreign Policy Analysis in the Asia Pacific: Rational Leaders and Risky Behavior*. New York, NY: Routledge.

Herrington, Luke M. 2011. "Why the Rise of China Will Not Lead to Global Hegemony". (http://www.e-ir.info/2011/07/15/why-the-precarious-rise-of-china-will-not-lead-to-global-hegemony/ accessed 16 October 2016).

Jeffery, Renée. 2009. "Evaluating the 'China threat': Power Transition Theory, the Successor-State Image and the Dangers of Historical Analogies". *Australian Journal of International Affairs* 63(2): 309–324.

Khoo, Nicholas. 2013. "China and Coexistence: Beijing's National Security Strategy for the Twenty-First Century". *Political Science Quarterly* 128(3): 543–45.

Kim, Woosang, and Scott Gates. 2015. "Power Transition Theory and the Rise of China." *International Area Studies Review* 18(3): 219–26.

Kissinger, Henry. 1957. *A World Restored: Castlereagh, Metternich, and the Problem of Peace, 1812–1822*. Boston, MA: Houghton Mifflin.

Kugler, Jacek, and Douglas Lemke (eds.). 1996. *Parity and War - Evaluations and Extensions of the War Ledger*. Ann Arbor, MI: University of Michigan Press.

Layne, Christopher. 2008. "China's Challenge to US Hegemony". *Current History* 107(705): 13–18.

Lee, Sang-Hwan. 2015. "Global and Regional Orders in the 21st Century in Terms of Multi-Layered Power Transition Theory: The cases of US-China and China-Japan Relations". *International Area Studies Review* 18(3): 266–279.

Legro, Jeffrey W. 2008. "Purpose Transitions: China's Rise and the American Response" in *China's Ascent: Power, Security, and the Future of International Politics*, edited by Robert S. Ross and Feng Zhu, 163–190. Ithaca, NY: Cornell University Press.

Lemke, Douglas. 2002. *Regions of War and Peace*. Cambridge: Cambridge University Press.

Lemke, Douglas. 2004. "Great Powers in the Post-Cold War World: a Power Transition Perspective" in *Balance of Power: Theory and Practice in the 21st Century*, edited by T. V. Paul, James J. Wirtz, and Michel Fortmann, 52–55. Stanford, CA: Stanford University Press.

Lemke, Douglas and Jacek Kugler. 1996. "The Evolution of the Power Transition Perspective" in *Parity and War – Evaluations and Extensions of the War Ledger*, edited by Jacek Kugler and Douglas Lemke, 3–34. Ann Arbor, MI: University of Michigan Press.

Lemke, Douglas, and Ronald L. Tammen. 2006. "Power Transition Theory and the Rise of China". *International Interactions* 29(4): 269–271.

Levy, Jack S. 2004. "What Do Great Powers Balance Against and When?" in *Balance of Power: Theory and Practice in the 21st Century*, edited by T. V. Paul, James J. Wirtz, and Michel Fortmann, 29–51. Stanford, CA: Stanford University Press.

Levy, Jack S. 2008. "Power Transition Theory and the Rise of China" in *China's Ascent - Power, Security, and the Future of International Politics*, edited by Robert S. Ross and Feng Zhu, 11–33. Ithaca, NY: Cornell University Press.

Liegl, Markus and Reinhard Wolf. 2016. "Home Alone? EUrope's Dilemmas in an Age of Growing Sino-American Rivalry." Paper presented at the 57th Annual Convention of the International Studies Association, 13–16 March 2016, Atlanta/Georgia USA.

Lim, Yves-Heng. 2014. "How (Dis)Satisfied is China? A power transition theory perspective". *Journal of Contemporary China* 24(92): 280–97.

Lobell, Steven E. 2016. "Realism, Balance of Power, and Power Transitions" in *Accommodating Rising Powers: Past, Present, and Future*, edited by T. V. Paul, 33–52. Cambridge: Cambridge University Press.

Mearsheimer, John J. 1993. "The Case for a Ukrainian Nuclear Deterrent". *Foreign Affairs* 72(3): 50–66.

Mearsheimer, John J. 2001. *The Tragedy of Great Power Politics*. New York, NY: Norton.

Mearsheimer, John J. 2014. "Why the Ukraine Crisis Is the West's Fault". *Foreign Affairs*.

Morgenthau, Hans J. 1954. *Politics Among Nations: The Struggle for Power and Peace*. New York: Knopf.

Motyl, Alexander J. 2015. "The Surrealism of Realism: Misreading the War in Ukraine". Accessed 30 May 2016. http://www.worldaffairsjournal.org/article/surrealism-realism-misreading-war-ukraine

Müller, Harald and Andreas Schmidt. 2009. Natural Friends? Relations between the United States and India after 2001 (PRIF Report 87). Frankfurt: Peace Research Institute Frankfurt.

Nolte, Detlef. 2010. "How to Compare Regional Powers: Analytical Concepts and Research Topics". *Review of International Studies* 36(4): 881–901.

Nossel, Suzanne. 2016. "The World's Rising Powers Have Fallen". (http://foreignpolicy.com/2016/07/06/brics-brazil-india-russia-china-south-africa-economics-recession Accessed 16 October 2016)

O'Neill, Jim and Anna Stupnytska. 2009. The Long-Term Outlook for the BRICs and N-11 Post Crisis. Global Economics Paper No. 192. London: Goldman Sachs.

Organski, A. F. K. 1958. *World Politics*. New York, NY: Knopf.

Organski, A. F. K. 1968. *World Politics – Second Edition. Borzoi Books in Political Science*. New York, NY: Knopf.

Organski, A. F. K. and Jacek Kugler. 1980. *The War Ledger*. Chicago, IL: University of Chicago Press.

Paul, T. V. 2004. "Introduction: The Enduring Axioms of Balance of Power Theory and Their Contemporary Relevance" in *Balance of Power: Theory and Practice in the 21st Century*, edited by T. V. Paul, James J. Wirtz, and Michel Fortmann. Stanford, CA: Stanford University Press.

Paul, T. V. 2016. "The Accommodation of Rising Powers in World Politics". In *Accommodating Rising Powers: Past, Present, and Future*, edited by T. V. Paul, 3–32. Cambridge: Cambridge University Press.

Paul, T. V. and Manesh Shankar. 2014. "Status Accommodation Through Institutional Means: India's Rise and the Global Order" in *Status in World Politics,* edited by T. V. Paul, Deborah W. Larson, and William C. Wohlforth, 165–191. New York, NY: Cambridge University Press.

Paul, T.V, James J. Wirtz, and M. Fortmann, eds. 2004. *Balance of Power: Theory and Practice in the 21st Century*. Stanford, CA: Stanford University Press.

Rauch, Carsten. 2008. Farewell Non-Alignment? Constancy and Change of Foreign Policy in Post-Colonial India (PRIF Report 85). Frankfurt: Peace Research Institute Frankfurt.

Rauch, Carsten. 2014. *Das Konzept des friedlichen Machtübergangs: Die Machtübergangstheorie und der weltpolitische Aufstieg Indiens*. Baden-Baden: Nomos.

Rauch, Carsten. 2016. "Adjusting Power Transition Theory – Satisfaction with the Status Quo, International Power Constellations, and the Case of the Weimar Republic". *Geopolitics, History, and International Relations* 8(2): 127–158.

Rynning, Sten, and Jens Ringsmose. 2008. "Why Are Revisionist States Revisionist? Reviving Classical Realism as an Approach to Understanding International Change". *International Politics* 45(1): 19–39.

Schweller, Randall L. 1994. "Bandwagoning for Profit: Bringing the Revisionist State Back in". *International Security* 19(1): 72–107.

Schweller, Randall L. 1998. *Deadly Imbalances: Tripolarity and Hitler's Strategy of World Conquest*. New York, NY: Columbia University Press.

Schweller, Randall L. 2008. *Unanswered Threats: Political Constraints on the Balance of Power*. Princeton, NJ: Princeton University Press.

Shirk, Susan L. 2007. *China: Fragile Superpower*. Oxford: Oxford University Press.

Silvius, Ray. 2014. "Emerging Powers in a Comparative Perspective. The Political and Economic Rise of the BRIC Countries". *Europe-Asia Studies* 66(8): 1383–5.

Siverson, Randolph M., and Ross A. Miller. 1996. "The Power Transition: Problems and Prospects" in *Parity and War: Evaluations and Extensions of the War Ledger*, edited by Jacek Kugler and Douglas Lemke, 57–73. Ann Arbor, MI: University of Michigan Press.

Sputnik News 2016. "Towards an Alliance? Current State and Prospects of Russia-China Friendship". (https://sputniknews.com/ politics/201608271044691247-russia-china-cooperation accessed on 16 October 2016)

Tammen, Ronald L., and Jacek Kugler. 2006. "Power Transition and China–US Conflicts". *Chinese Journal of International Politics* 1(1): 35–55.

Tammen, Ronald L., Jacek Kugler, Douglas Lemke, Allan C. Stamm, III, Mark Abdollahian, Carole Alsharabati, Brian Efrid, and A. F. K. Organski. 2000. *Power Transitions: Strategies for the 21st Century*. New York, NY: Seven Bridges Press.

van Agtmael, Antoine. 2012. "Think Again: The BRICS". Accessed 16 October 2016. http://foreignpolicy.com/2012/10/08/think-again-the-brics

Walt, Stephen M. 1987. *The Origins of Alliances*. Ithaca, NY: Cornell University Press.

Waltz, Kenneth N. 1979. *Theory of International Politics*. New York, NY: McGraw-Hill.

Waltz, Kenneth N. 2008. "Realist Thought and Neorealist Theory" in *Realism and International Politics*, edited by Kenneth N. Waltz, 67–82. New York, NY: Routledge.

Wohlforth, William C. 2011. "Gilpinian Realism and International Relations". *International Relations* 25(4): 499–511.

Wolfers, Arnold. 1962. *Discord and Collaboration: Essays on International Politics*. Baltimore, MD: Johns Hopkins University Press.

6

China's Military Modernisation: International Systemic Change through Internal Balancing?

LAYLA DAWOOD

By balance of power, scholars frequently mean the systemic situation or condition in which an objective equilibrium of power is observed among the major units of a given international system, power being understood in terms of material resources (especially military capabilities).[1] The term can also refer to a policy or a principle that guides policy formulation. Balancing policies and behaviours are related to the expectation that systems' units will act to prevent the formation of concentrations of power and that states will counteract concentrations already formed.

Accordingly, balancing can take two main forms: *internal balancing* and *external balancing*. The employment of the first concept often implies economic, technological and especially military efforts taken by a state using its own means to counter the accumulation of military capabilities by a possible opponent; the second refers to the creation of military alliances to deal with the possibility of war (Waltz 1979). Nonetheless, scholars diverge when empirically identifying balancing behaviours (Martin 1999, 2003; Nexon 2009).

As a systemic theory, Waltz's balance of power theory (1979) focused on

---

[1]   This being the case, the opposite systemic situation involves the concentration of power by a single actor, which can take the form of unipolarity (when there is an especially powerful actor in the system), hegemony (when international rules are determined by a single actor) or empire (when the less powerful units lose autonomy to the most powerful) (Nexon 2009, 334–5).

explaining the tendency of international systems to bipolar and multipolar equilibriums, but did not produce a thorough characterisation of balancing behaviours. In turn, theories of balancing have sought to explain the conditions under which states will engage in balancing policies, trying to establish which states are most likely to balance (Nexon, 2009).[2]

Nevertheless, balance of power theories fail to clearly specify how balancing can be empirically identified, and when they attempt to do so, they focus on external balancing (i.e. the formation of alliances) to the detriment of internal balancing. Exemplifying the focus on external balancing, Kaufman and Wohlforth (2007) and Wohlforth et al. (2007) undertook a series of tests to verify the capacity of balance of power theories to explain systemic change. The scholars analysed the rise and fall of previous unipolar systems to verify the concrete operation of the balance of power theory's expectations. In short, in opposition to balancing predicted by the balance of power theory as the cause of transformation of unipolar systems, Kaufman and Wohlforth (2007) maintain that the final collapse of past unipolarities is more properly understood as resulting from the classical effects of imperial overstretch.[3] In addition, Wohlforth et al. (2007) affirm that balancing occurs, and that it can be an important phenomenon, but its effects are minimised by collective action problems in the formation of alliances and by domestic obstacles to emulating the pole´s advances (thus hampering internal balancing).

At first glance, these works suggest that unipolar systems cannot be transformed by means of balancing and that imperial overstretch is a better way of explaining hegemons' decline. In contrast, this chapter argues that these scholars have primarily signalised that alliances (external balancing) were historically ineffective in producing systemic balance in unipolar systems. Nevertheless, the process of internal balancing should not be discarded by the specialised literature as a source of international systemic change.

In sum, this chapter intends to contribute to the debate concerning the current state of Realism by exploring an underdeveloped realist concept: internal balancing. Subsequently, China's rise, more specifically the recent naval modernisation efforts, will be analysed as a possible illustrative case of internal balancing. The chapter tests the hypothesis that China is changing the current unipolar systems by means of internally balancing the US.

---

[2]   For examples of this kind of theory, see the works of Walt (1990), Schweller (1994) and Christensen and Snyder (1990), who elaborate on the frequency of balancing behaviour and the conditions under which it is expected to occur.

[3]   Imperial overstretch refers to the loss of economic dynamism and the consequent decline of a hegemon due to excessive spending on defence (Wohlforth 1999).

Towards a Theoretical Model of Internal Balancing

The primary aim here is to develop criteria to identify global internal balancing, that is, balancing pursued against the United States, the sole pole of the international system inaugurated with the fall of the USSR. Balancing can also happen at a regional level, but since the purpose of this chapter is to verify if the whole system is changing by means of internal balancing, it is important to design ways to differentiate among efforts forged to counter regional enemies and efforts that deal with the unipole. Accordingly, internal balancing is here considered as a process comprising a group of behaviours that do not need to be consciously directed to forge equilibrium but that must have the potential to do so. Moreover, the effective accomplishment of global systemic balance cannot be used as a criterion to identify global balancing practices. This would neglect the possibility that both effective and ineffective balancing behaviours could take place.

With that in mind, this chapter argues that global internal balancing (that is, balancing directed towards the poles of a system) refers to a process comprising a group of actions which, over the years, have the potential to reduce the capabilities gap between the balancer and existing opponent poles. In the current unipolar system, to qualify as global internal balancing, a group of behaviours must increase the balancer's capabilities to deal with the US in case of a major war. Obviously, the same efforts and capabilities used to balance the US could also help the balancer deal with other possible regional adversaries. By major war, this chapter means a war involving vital interests of all sides, that is: a war of life and death to all parties.

Therefore, internal balancing has an essential military component, which increases the balancer's capabilities to either attack an existing pole or to defend itself against it. However, there is another important component of this process, which helps to differentiate balancing behaviours from ordinary defence improvements: the concomitant rise of economic and political capabilities (e.g. the economic growth of a country and the improvement of central government ability to impose internal taxes and transform private gains in public goods). Economic and political capabilities do not, by themselves, immediately increase a balancer's capabilities to win a war, but they make victory possible by generating resources needed to invest in military capabilities.

When carried out by states that qualify as *poles* in multipolar and bipolar systems, internal balancing can lead to various results. When it is unsuccessfully performed, it might transform bipolar systems into unipolarities and multipolar systems into bipolarities due to the decline of the state which failed to balance. In contrast, when successful, it can guarantee the maintenance of the systemic balance, in which case no systemic change is observed since equilibrium is preserved. It can also lead to the disproportional rise of the balancing pole contributing to the decay of its opponent, either because the latter cannot keep up with the pace of investments in defence or because it eventually loses a war for lack of military capabilities.

In turn, in unipolar systems, when successfully carried out by a *pole candidate*, internal balancing can change the system when it equalises a balancer's capabilities with the current pole(s), consequently changing the system's polarity (from unipolar to bipolar, or from bipolar to multipolar). When internal balancing is successful, a pole candidate not only becomes better at defending itself against an enemy, but becomes able to potentially win a major armed conflict against current global powers. And, to win a major conflict, weapons are of course needed, but so are economic and political capabilities to sustain investments in military capabilities in times of war and peace.[4]

To sum up, the internal balancing model herein developed assumes that the continued economic and political improvements achieved by a pole or a pole candidate (and the maintenance of these achievements in time) enable the occurrence and continuation of the second component of the internal balancing process (which is military in nature). In addition, successful internal balancing necessarily comprises a military build-up which increases the balancer's prospects of winning a major war against the pole(s) of a system.

---

[4]   In this respect, various theories drive attention to different domestic and economic features which inspire the characterisation of the first component of the model on the global internal balancing process. Power Transition Theory (PTT) stresses that transformations in productivity and population are related to the rise of global powers and Gilpin (2002) drives attention to transformations in sectors such as transportation, communications, and in the economic system itself. In addition, Long Leadership Cycle Theory (LLCT) highlights the causal relation between economic innovations and the rise and fall of great powers. According to the supporters of this last theory, the rise of a dominant power is the result of some sort of invention related to the leading sectors of world economy which provides the inventor with the sort of advantages that usually derive from monopolies. In contrast, the decline of a dominant power is caused by the diffusion of its economic innovations to other states (Rasler and Thompson 1994; Tammen et al. 2000). In terms of political features, PTT and Gilpin (2002) work with the concept of political capacity, which relates to the distinction between state power and national power: the latter being the sum of a country's assets and the former being comprised by what state authorities can really use for public purposes. As indicators of political capacity, PTT suggests the use of fiscal and tax policy numbers.

Finally, to deal with an opponent pole's military capabilities, a balancer might choose a combination of the following behaviours: 1) off-setting – which refers to an increase in the number or quality of weapons already at the disposal of the balancer; 2) emulation – to copy or to reproduce the opponent's capabilities; and/or 3) innovation – to come up with new capabilities that help counter the ones owned by a potential opponent (Elman 1999; Resende-Santos 2007; Taliaferro 2007).

This chapter focuses on the second component of the internal balancing phenomenon: it verifies if the Chinese military modernisation efforts count as internal balancing and if these behaviours have been effective in changing the current international system[5].

Is China Internally Balancing the US?

China and the US disagree especially in what concerns the Taiwan issue and America's influence over seas and oceans near China. Therefore, Chinese authorities have been trying to improve their naval capabilities, which would be essential to respond to the set of capabilities at the disposal of the US in case of a war in Asia (O'Rourke 2012). In view of the Chinese current focus on naval capabilities[6], this chapter attempts to check if these modernisation efforts provide China with better chances of victory in case of an armed conflict against the US. In other words, the next sections verify if the Chinese naval improvements can be understood as internal balancing and analyse if these behaviours have the potential to change the current unipolar system.

The naval capabilities acquired by China during the 1990s and 2000s reflect a new emphasis by the Chinese authorities and scholars on the development of naval power.[7] China's naval modernisation began during the 1990s and was

---

[5]   For the complete test of this model against China's economic, political and military rise, see Dawood (2013).

[6]   This does not mean that naval modernisation is China's sole means of balancing. Nonetheless, this chapter concentrates on naval modernisation due to the attention the Chinese government has been giving to these efforts.

[7]   Surely, this new focus would be better characterised if one could show increases in naval spending over the years, but no official breakdown of defence spending by service is available for China. However, various Chinese publications seem to confirm this new emphasis. According to Fravel and Liebman (2011), Chinese navy officials are increasingly casting the PLAN (People's Liberation Army Navy) as the protector of China's economy. It is often argued that the heart of China's economy is more and more concentrated in coastal areas and that China's dependence on maritime shipping is growing, turning the protection of China's sea lines of communication (SLOCs) to a priority (Fravel and Liebman 2011, 74–5). Chinese official sources also point to this new focus. A White Paper published in 2006 states that the country aims at extending

boosted after 1996, when the United States deployed two aircraft carriers to Taiwan's surroundings in response to Chinese missile tests and naval exercises near Taiwan (Cole 2009, 2010). The modernisation efforts 'comprise a broad array of weapon acquisition programs, including programs for anti-ship ballistic missiles (ASBMs), anti-ship cruise missiles (ASCMs), land-attack cruise missiles (LACMs), surface-to-air missiles, mines, manned aircraft, unmanned aircraft, submarines, aircraft carriers, destroyers, frigates, patrol craft, amphibious ships, mine countermeasures (MCM) ships, hospital ships, and supporting C4IS[8] (O'Rourke 2012, 3).

Particularly, new submarine building programs contributed to significant changes in the composition of China's naval force during the past two decades. China went from having two modern attack submarines in 1995 to 39 in 2014. The new submarines are regarded as quieter and, consequently, less detectable (O'Rourke 2016, 16).

There is a long-lasting Russian influence on the Chinese navy, especially in terms of the design of its vessels. However, the Chinese are reportedly seeking to emulate the US naval warfare network.[9] For that purpose, investments have been made on enhancing information technology and PLAN's communications capabilities. Improvements can be identified in relation to the construction of a national fibre optics network and of space-based C4ISR capabilities (Erickson and Chase 2008, 25).

Nevertheless, a technological innovation, the ASBM, might aid the Chinese to perform its sea-denial strategy, permitting China to use ballistic missiles to attack moving surface warships. Traditionally, ballistic missiles were not considered efficient against ships at sea since ships are moving targets and

---

the strategic depth of offshore defensive operations and at enhancing its capabilities in integrated maritime operations. Another White Paper published in 2008 for the first time referred to the ground forces as a service equivalent to the navy, air force, and second artillery. It emphasises the objective of developing the navy's capabilities to conduct cooperation in distant waters (Erickson and Goldstein 2009, 47–8; Hartnett and Vellucci 2011). In 2013, a new White Paper stated the objective to develop blue water capabilities (the capability to operate globally, that is in open oceans and deep waters) (O'Rourke 2016).

[8]   C4IS stands for Command, Control, Communications, and Computers Information System.

[9]   In defining network centric warfare, scholars emphasise the use of new technologies to produce information and improve results in war. In other words, there is a focus on 'the new technologies used to create more effective sensor and communications architectures. These architectures, it is argued, will enable us to create and exploit a common situational awareness, increase our speed of command, and "get inside the enemy's OODA [observe, orient, decide, and act] loop"' (Smith 2001, 59).

missiles, once fired, could not change trajectory to account for target motion. However, the PLA is reportedly trying to place seekers in high-explosive missile warheads that would activate as the warhead descends into the target area and guide the warhead to the moving ship. If the Chinese succeed in achieving such innovation, it could pose a huge challenge to US forces (McDevitt 2011).

Therefore, the behaviours of *offsetting* (represented by the acquisition of more submarines, frigates and destroyers), *emulation* (of an American networked fleet, for instance) and military innovation (the creation of anti-ship ballistic missiles) seem to be present when Chinese modernisation efforts are analysed.

However, for this chapter, it is important to inquire whether these modernisation efforts are enough to qualify as internal balancing against the US. For that, a comparison between the Chinese and the American navies is in order. Navies should not be compared only in terms of capabilities, but also in terms of preparedness to fulfil their missions and objectives (O'Rourke 2012, 36). Chinese military observers such as McDevitt (2011) and Shlapak et al. (2009) claim that the near-term objective of China's naval military modernisation efforts is to improve this country's ability to deal with the Taiwan issue in case it turns into an armed conflict with the US. To prepare against American interference in a conflict with Taiwan, naval power seems indispensable to China since the US would use its own maritime capabilities to deal with China. Accordingly, China is believed to be adopting an anti-access strategy, which aims at deterring or at least delaying a potential US intervention in a conflict between China and Taiwan.[10]

This sea denial strategy is also referred to as near-seas active defence (in opposition to the near-coast defence strategy adopted during the Cold War) since the aim is to cover a much larger sea area than the coast. The near-seas active defence covers the first island chain (which stretches from the Kurile Islands through the islands of Japan, the Ryukyu Archipelago, Taiwan and the Philippines to Borneo Island), the Yellow Sea, East China Sea, and South China Sea, sea areas adjacent to the outer rims of this island chain and those of the North Pacific. The concept does not cover the South Pacific and the Indian Ocean (Li 2011, 116).

---

[10] It is important to emphasise that 'anti-access' and 'area denial' are US terms and not Chinese ones. Those terms, first employed by the US Department of Defense in the 2001 Quadrennial Defense Review, are often used interchangeably by analysts to characterise the attempt to prevent a US military intervention if China attacks Taiwan. In particular, the assumed Chinese objective is to impede US aircraft carriers from getting within tactical aircraft operating distance from China (McDevitt 2011, 192).

The submarine forces are the most important PLAN (People's Liberation Army Navy) capability to perform the sea-denial strategy. Assuming it takes three submarines to keep one on station (one on station, one going home, one getting ready to go), McDevitt (2011) estimates that a sea-denial strategy requires around 60 to 75 modern submarines to deal with US carriers. The PLAN has currently 39 modern attack boats. That means that it is not unequivocal that China's forces can effectively perform the strategy of sea-denial (McDevitt 2011, O'Rourke 2016).

On the other hand, in terms of far seas operations, China has been slow to increase its navy's ability to remain at sea for extended periods. At the same time, it has been working to overcome some of its limitations. In 2013, two new FUCHI replenishment oilers were added to the force. These ships rotate in support of Gulf of Aden (GOA) counter-piracy deployments. Also, the amphibious force is being modernised; yet China has not significantly expanded its capacity in this area yet.

Concerning the acquisition of foreign bases, observers such as Khurana (2008) have stated that China is building a series of bases in the Indian Ocean to support Chinese naval operations along the sea line of communication linking China to the oil sources of the Persian Gulf, which has been referred to as a 'string of pearls'[11]. However, this information is disputed by analysts such as Kostecka (2011) and Erickson (2010) who argue that China has built commercial port facilities in the Indian Ocean, but not naval bases. These scholars claim that China is pursuing a strategy of having 'places not bases', which involves diplomatic agreements with other states' governments that allow access to their facilities to obtain essential supplies, such as fuel, food, and freshwater for deployed forces. Such agreements can also involve reciprocal guarantees of military support in such areas as training, equipment, and education. In other words, China is seeking to guarantee that its navy would have places to visit, not staying permanently anywhere abroad.

Conclusion

In conclusion, the behaviours which are part of the military component of the internal balancing process (off-setting, emulation and/or military innovation) can be identified among China's naval modernisation efforts. Moreover, the timing of China's actions in what regards naval capabilities indicates a correlation between the Chinese naval modernisation and US unipolarity.

---

[11]   This theory was a creation of a 2004 study commissioned by the US Department of Defense entitled *Energy Futures in Asia* and is broadly accepted as true in the US and India.

Although China is not simply emulating American naval capabilities, it seems to be trying to offset American naval power through the adoption of an anti-access strategy greatly based on submarine war.

Nonetheless, it is not clear if all the criteria herein proposed to qualify a group of actions as internal balancing are met: Chinese efforts are potentially directed at diminishing the gap between the US and China's capabilities, but the Chinese efforts do not considerably increase its chances of winning a major war against the US. Nevertheless, Chinese maritime modernisation efforts have improved its ability to deter a possible US intervention in the Taiwan Strait. If a war breaks out near Taiwan, Chinese capabilities might be enough to coerce the US out of this conflict, especially in case the American authorities do not consider the defence of Taiwan as a vital American interest. Nonetheless, naval modernisation still fails to provide China with the resources necessary to project power outside the so called 'first island chain'. Particularly, China has the disadvantage of relying on SLOCs for vital products such as energy sources. Consequently, the capability of protecting its SLOC is essential to raise China's chances of winning a major war against the US, since the latter, in case its vital interests were at risk, could impose a naval embargo on China that would damage Chinese war efforts, making victory a lot harder.

In a nutshell, China's naval force modernisation, at most, enables China to win a war over Taiwan, but not enough efforts are being taken to enable China to win a conflict farther in Asia. In other words, modernisation efforts seem not to be sufficient to guarantee victory on a major conflict, that is, a conflict over which the unipole would be willing to use all its resources to win.

Therefore, China's efforts to acquire adequate capabilities to perform a sea-denial strategy are only consistent with an early stage of the internal balancing process. An unequivocal internal balancing movement would necessarily encompass the acquisition of capabilities to protect China's SLOCs and/or to project power beyond the near seas. To the extent that balancing is already occurring, it has been inefficient in changing the current unipolar system. This means there are no empirical signs to support the hypothesis that guided this study; consequently, internal balancing cannot yet be said to be changing the current international system.

In sum, realist balance of power theory remains challenged in its capacity to explain systemic change. Nonetheless, this research does not necessarily refute the theory: there is no evidence to support the claim that internal balancing will not change unipolarity in the long run. Future research should explore why internal balancing has been slow in the current unipolar system.

Author note: This chapter is a result of my PhD studies pursued at the Catholic University of Rio de Janeiro (PUC-Rio). I would like to express gratitude to Professor João Pontes Nogueira (PUC-Rio) and Professor William Wohlforth (Dartmouth College) for the supervision of this work, as well as to the Brazilian public agencies CAPES, CNPQ and FAPERJ for the funding provided during my PhD.

References

Christensen, Thomas. J. and Jack Snyder. 1990. "Chain Gangs and Passed Bucks: Predicting Alliance Patterns in Multipolarity". *International Organization* 4: 137–168.

Cole, Bernard. 2009. "More Red than Expert: Chinese Sea Power During the Cold War" in *China Goes to Sea: Maritime Transformation in Comparative Historical Perspective*, edited by Andrew S. Erickson, Lyle J. Goldstein, and Carnes Lord, 320–340. Annapolis: Naval Institute Press.

Cole, Bernard D. 2010. *The Great Wall at Sea: China's Navy in the Twenty-first Century*. 2nd ed. Annapolis: Naval Institute Press.

Dawood, Layla I. A. 2013. "China versus the United States: Is Bipolarity Back? A Study of Internal Balancing as a Possible Source of International Systemic Change". PhD dissertation, Pontifícia Universidade Católica do Rio de Janeiro.

Elman, Colin. 1999. "The Logic of Emulation: The Diffusion of Military Practices in the International System". PhD dissertation, Columbia University.

Erickson, Andrew S., and Michael S. Chase. 2008. "Information technology and China's Naval Modernization". *Joint Force Quarterly* 50: 24–30.

Erickson, Andrew S., and Lyle S. Goldstein. 2009. "Gunboats for China's New Grand Canals? Probing the Intersection of Beijing's Naval and Oil Security Policies". *Naval War College Review* 62(2): 43–76.

Erickson, Andrew S. 2010. "Chinese Sea Power in Action: The Counter-Piracy Mission in the Gulf of Aden and Beyond". In *The PLA at Home and Abroad: Assessing the Operational Capabilities of China's Military*, edited by Roy Kamphausen, David Lai, and Andrew Scobell, 295–376. (http://www.StrategicStudiesInstitute.army.mil/ accessed on 31 May 2012).

Fravel, Taylor M. and Alexander Liebman. 2011. "Beyond the Moat: The PLAN's Evolving Interests and Potential Influence" in *The Chinese Navy: Expanding Capabilities, Evolving Roles*, edited by P. C. Saunders et al., 41–80. Washington: National University Press.

Gilpin, Robert. 2002. *War and Change in World Politics*. New York: Cambridge University Press.

Hartnett, Daniel M. and Frederic Vellucci. 2011. "Toward a Maritime Security Strategy: An Analysis of Chinese Views since the early 1990's" in *The Chinese Navy: Expanding Capabilities, Evolving Roles*, edited by P. C. Saunders et al., 81–108. Washington: National Defense University Press.

Kaufman, Stuart J. and William C. Wohlforth. 2007. "Balancing and Balancing Failure in Biblical Times: Assyria and the Ancient Middle Eastern System, 900–600 BCE" in *The Balance of Power in World History*, edited by Stuart Kaufman, Richard Little and William Wohlforth, 22–46. New York: Palgrave Macmillan.

Kostecka, Daniel J. 2011. "Places and Bases: The Chinese Navy's Emerging Support Network in the Indian Ocean". *Naval War College Review* 64(1): 59–78.

Khurana, Gurpreet S. 2008. "China's 'String of Pearls' in the Indian Ocean and its Security Implications". *Strategic Analysis*, 32(1): 1–39.

Li, Nan. 2011. "The Evolution of China's Naval Strategy and Capabilities: from "Near Coast" and "Near Seas" to "Far Seas" in *The Chinese Navy: Expanding Capabilities, Evolving Roles*, edited by P. C. Saunders et al., 109–140. Washington: National Defense University Press.

McDevitt, Michael. 2011. "The PLA Navy's Anti-access Role in a Taiwan Contingency" in *The Chinese Navy: Expanding Capabilities, Evolving Roles*, edited by P. C. Saunders et al., 191–214. Washington: National Defense University Press.

Martin, Susan B. 1999. Balances of Power versus Balancing: a Conceptual Analysis. Working Paper. Christopher H. Browne Center for International Politics, University of Pennsylvania. (http://www.sas.upenn.edu/penncip/Reports/BOPVBAL.htm accessed 31/05/2017)

Martin, Susan B. 2003. "From Balance of Power to Balancing Behavior: The Long and Winding Road" in *Perspectives on Structural Realism*, edited by A. Hanami, 61–82. New York: Palgrave Macmillan.

Nexon, Daniel. H. 2009. "The Balance of Power in the Balance". *World Politics* 61(2): 330–359.

O'Rourke, Ronald. 2012. China Naval Modernization: Implications for U.S. Navy Capabilities – Background and Issues for Congress. CRS, 23 March. (http://www.dtic.mil/get-tr-doc/pdf?AD=ADA559840 accessed on 31/05/2017)

O'Rourke, Ronald. 2016. China Naval Modernization: Implications for U.S. Navy Capabilities – Background and Issues for Congress. CRS, 31 March. (https://news.usni.org/wp-content/uploads/2016/06/RL33153.pdf accessed on 31/05/2017)

Rasler, Karen A. and William R. Thompson. 1994. *The Great Powers and Global Struggle. 1490–1990*. Lexington: The University Press of Kentucky.

Resende-Santos, João. 2007. *Neorealism, States, and the Modern Mass Army*. Cambridge: Cambridge University Press.

Shlapak, David et al. 2009. *A Question of Balance: Political Context and Military Aspects of the China-Taiwan Dispute*. Santa Monica: RAND.

Schweller, Randall. L. 1994. "Bandwagoning for Profit: Bringing the Revisionist State Back in". *International Security* 19: 72–107.

Smith, Edward. 2001. "Network-centric warfare. What is the point?". *Naval War College Review* 1(1): 59–75.

Taliaferro, Jeffrey W. 2007. "State Building for Future Wars: Neoclassical Realism and the Resource-extractive State". *Global Review* (Trial Issue): 128–165.

Tammen, Ronald et al. 2000. *Power Transitions. Strategies for the 21st Century*. New York: Chatham House Publishers.

Walt, Stephen. M. 1990. The Origins of Alliances. Ithaca: Cornell University Press.

Waltz, Kenneth. 1979. *Theory of International Politics*. New York: McGraw-Hill.

Wohlforth, William C. 1999. "The Stability of a Unipolar World". *International Security*, 24(1): 5–41.

Wohlforth, William C. et al. 2007. "Testing Balance of Power Theory in World History". *European Journal of International Relations* 13(2): 155–185.

7

Realism and Cyber Conflict: Security in the Digital Age

ANTHONY J.S. CRAIG & BRANDON VALERIANO

With the proliferation of Information and Communication Technologies (ICTs), cyber security has become both a major source of concern for policy-makers and of great interest to scholars of international relations. From the financial loss to businesses through cyber crime, the theft of classified government data, or the targeting of critical infrastructure, cyber security poses a significant challenge to the economic and national security of countries globally. Cyberspace is now considered the fifth domain of warfare after land, sea, air, and space (Economist 2010), and traditional frameworks can help us understand this relatively new form of conflict.

Realism has long been a dominant paradigm in the international relations ficld and is based on a general set of assumptions about international politics: that states are the most important actors, who operate as independent units within an international system lacking centralised authority, and rationally pursue their self-interest to assure power and security (Schmidt 2002, 9). The emerging cyber security field exhibits a resurgence of realist-influenced perspectives with a focus on security and competition, the distribution of power, the advantage of offence over defence, and the benefits of deterrence strategies, thus offering an opportunity to evaluate realism's role in these debates.

In this chapter, we appraise the utility of realism in explaining international cyber politics. We provide an overview of realist theory and how it relates to cyber security before addressing a set of specific realist-influenced topics within the current cyber security discourse. By evaluating the evidence surrounding each, we assess the relevance of realism as a descriptive and prescriptive theory of state behaviour in the cyber domain. We argue that, although realism can help in raising key issues in cyber security, overall the perspective lacks the ability to explain the dynamics of cyber conflict.

Realism and Cyber Security

The realist tradition can be traced back to Thucydides' analysis of the Peloponnesian War in the 5th century BCE where he emphasised the amoral nature of international politics and the importance of power to political survival (Vasquez 1995, 9–19). However, its articulation into a distinct theory of international relations can be attributed largely to Hans Morgenthau (1948) who focused on the struggle for power between rationally-acting, self-interested states.

Within neorealism, established in the 1970s, there is a divide between defensive and offensive realism. Both agree that survival is the state's primary motive, but for defensive realists, most states are status quo powers that aim towards a balance of power thereby maintaining a stable international system (Waltz 1979). Offensive realists, on the other hand, argue that states aim to maximise their power to ensure their survival in an anarchical system (Mearsheimer 2001). The most recent strand of realism, neoclassical realism, explains state behaviour not purely on structural factors, but also domestic level variables including the perceptions and misperceptions of decision makers (Ripsman et al. 2016).

Realism has been challenged for its inability to explain state behaviour or offer productive policy guidance. For example, several studies point to the lack of evidence that states act in accordance with balance of power logic, a prominent hypothesis within the realist literature (Rosecrance and Stein 1993, 10, 17–21; Schroeder 1994). Its contradictory predictions and lack of empirical progress leads Vasquez (1997) to condemn realism as a 'degenerative' rather than 'progressive' paradigm. Furthermore, statistical studies suggest the factors that realists argue increase national security, such as military build-ups and alliances, are often counterproductive and increase the likelihood of conflict (Senese and Vasquez 2008). Nevertheless, with its focus on security and conflict issues, realism appears to be the natural go-to theory for elucidating pressing cyber security issues.

The study of cyber conflict is generally thought to have begun when Arquilla and Ronfeldt (1993) developed the concepts of 'cyberwar' and 'netwar' and predicted a transformation of warfare in line with rapid advances in ICT. This form of conflict takes place within cyberspace, an environment defined simply as 'all of the computer networks in the world and everything they connect and control' (Clarke and Knake 2010, 70). Cyber conflict refers to 'the use of computational technologies in cyberspace for malevolent and/or destructive purposes in order to impact, change, or modify diplomatic and military interactions between entities' (Valeriano and Maness 2015, 32). It is these politically motivated types of interactions that we focus on because they directly impact national security.

Cyber threats are today perceived as a top national security concern as governments warn against attacks against vulnerable critical infrastructure. In 2012, for instance, the then US Defence Secretary warned of a cyber 'Pearl Harbor' against the power grid or the financial system, both of which are reliant on computer networks for their operation (Bumiller and Shanker 2012). According to a 2016 survey, 73 percent of Americans believed cyber terrorism presented a 'critical threat' to the United States (McCarthy 2016). Some commentators such as Clarke and Knake (2012) agree that cyberwar is a very real and pressing threat to national security, yet several scholars argue, to the contrary, that the threat is exaggerated. Rid (2013) writes that cyber war does not represent true violence in the Clausewitzian sense and is unlikely to in the future, while Valeriano and Maness (2015) demonstrate empirically the rare incidence and low severity of cyber conflict between rival states. Others have used securitisation theory to explain the heightened threat perception we currently witness (Cavelty 2008; Hansen and Nissenbaum 2009).

Realism is considered a useful framework by some for understanding cyberspace. As Reardon and Choucri (2012, 6) write: 'realist theories of deterrence, crisis management, and conflict may be used to understand whether cyberspace is stabilising or destabilising, whether cyber technologies will be a new source of conflict or of peace, and whether states will engage in cyber arms racing.' The rest of this chapter considers specific realist-informed issues in cyberspace and evaluates their relevance.

Anarchy and Security Competition in Cyberspace

Anarchy is the fundamental assumption underlying structural realist theories and refers to the lack of overarching authority to police the international system which instils a sense of distrust among states (Waltz 1979). This forces states to rely on self-help measures to achieve security or pursue their interests. For defensive realists, much of the causes of conflict arise from the competition between security-seeking states. The security dilemma describes the phenomenon whereby 'many of the means by which a state tries to increase its security decrease the security of others' (Jervis 1978, 169). Actions such as military build-ups or alliance making are often perceived as threats by other states who then take similar measures to enhance their own security; this process is often termed the spiral model with each action forcing a reaction (Glaser 2004, 44). The spiral model is at the heart of traditional conceptualisations of an escalating arms race which are said to cause rapid shifts in the balance of power, an increase in international tension, and a greater risk of miscalculation and conflict (Richardson 1960; Vasquez 1993).

In many ways, anarchy and its effects describe cyberspace well. Liberal IR theorists argue that the dangerous effects of anarchy can be ameliorated by global institutions which mediate interstate disputes and reduce uncertainty through increased information (Russett and Oneal 2001, 163–4). However, the cyber domain lacks effective global institutional governance. Relevant organisations include the International Telecommunications Union (ITU) and the Internet Corporation for Assigned Names and Numbers (ICANN), but their functions and competencies do not extend to conflict management.

Media reports of a cyber arms race are frequent (Paletta et al. 2015; Corera 2015), and this increased militarisation of cyberspace is evident through the creation of new military organisations, the drafting of cyber-military doctrines, the increase in cyber security budgets, and the hiring of cyber 'warriors' (Craig and Valeriano 2016a). A more secretive development is the suggested stockpiling of malicious code which can be used as weapons (Rid and McBurney 2012). Furthermore, Craig and Valeriano (2016a) provide empirical evidence demonstrating a relationship between build-ups in cyber capabilities and mutual perceptions of threat and competition between states in a select number of cases.

Realism can help explain the source of cyber arms racing behaviour as a response to threat in an anarchic world. Jervis (1978, 187–194) notes that the security dilemma is at its most intense when a build-up in offensive capabilities is more cost-effective than a build-up in defensive capabilities. The security dilemma is also more severe when offensive and defensive capabilities are indistinguishable. If so, states are unable to signal benign intentions and any build up in capability will be seen as a potential threat (199–206). In cyberspace, capabilities are very difficult to distinguish. For one, it is impossible to verify the offensive zero day exploits governments possess since they are, by definition, unknown. Moreover, cyber military organisations like US Cyber Command tend to have both defensive and offensive roles and if they are said to be increasing their budgets or personnel it is not obvious whether an offensive or defensive investment is being made. This fuels uncertainty and competition between states as they seek security in cyberspace.

For some realists, arms races increase the likelihood of war (Jervis 1978,

188; Van Evera 1998, 13), yet for others, military build-ups are a necessary means of deterring a revisionist power (Glaser 2004). A critical question is therefore whether security competition will escalate to actual conflict. Previous scholarship has demonstrated a relationship between arms races and both militarised interstate disputes and war (Sample 1997; Gibler et al. 2005). The concern here is whether cyber arms races will lead to a similar outcome. As Lord and Sharp (2011, 29) argue: 'conflict in cyberspace is uniquely predisposed to escalation given uncertainties about what constitutes an act of war and the growing number of state and non-state actors seeking offensive capabilities.'

The empirical record, however, suggests that although cyber conflict is becoming more frequent, this increase correlates with low level disruption and espionage tactics rather than more destructive forms of cyber warfare (Jensen, Maness, and Valeriano 2016, 17). Moreover, the data shows that cyber disputes are very unlikely to spill over into the physical domains of warfare suggesting that, rather than escalation, the prevailing trend is one of restraint (Valeriano and Maness 2016). Rather than live up to the predictions of the realist-informed spiral model, states appear to avoid escalation into warfare and restraint appears to be the prevailing norm instead. It may be too early to tell whether escalation may become a future trend, but thirty years of digital conflict demonstrate a remarkable degree of self-restraint in that states have avoided outright destruction and violence in cyberspace.

Cyber Power

Power is central to realism because it can ensure the independence and survival of the state in a self-help environment (Mearsheimer 2006, 79–81). As Morgenthau (1948, 13) claims: 'whatever the ultimate aim of international politics, power is always the immediate aim.' Realists often equate power to the state's assets such as the natural resources, industrial capacity, military strength, and population a state possesses (Morgenthau 1948, 80–108). The distribution of such capabilities among states is considered to have significant implications for stability in the international system. For instance, a longstanding debate has been whether a multipolar, bipolar, or unipolar power configuration creates a more peaceful world (Mearsheimer 2006, 78–80).

Cyber power is defined by Nye (2011, 123) as 'the ability to obtain preferred outcomes through use of the electronically interconnected information resources of the cyber domain', and its potential to transform international relations has become a prominent debate. Although there is no theory of cyber power within the realist literature, realism offers a framework to think about the distribution of power between actors and how this relates to conflict.

A core assumption of realism is that states are the most powerful and therefore most important actors in international politics. The information revolution challenges the primacy of the state, however, due to the greater involvement of non-state actors threatening traditional power dynamics (Eriksson and Giacomello 2006, 229). Non-state actors are increasingly important in international relations as Nye's (1990, 160) theory of power diffusion argues, and this is especially true in the cyber domain in which individual criminals, organisations, and terrorist groups can take advantage of the accessibility of the internet to threaten the dominance of the state, and where private firms play a role, both as providers of security and as sources of vulnerability.

We should not overstate this issue though because states are still the most dominant actors when it comes to cyber conflict. Non-state actors and terrorists do play a role, but their tactics have generally been ineffective or used as cover for nation-states seeking to hide their actions (Valeriano and Maness 2015, 164–187). It appears that states remain ultimately best placed to leverage the tools of cyber warfare with resources to invest in the manpower, research and development, and education that are unlikely to be rivalled by non-state actors.

It is hypothesised that due to the relative low cost of entry into the cyber warfare domain, traditionally weaker states challenge stronger states and reconfigure the power distribution in the system (Lango 2016, 12). For example, much attention has been paid to North Korea's training of thousands of hackers (Mulrine 2015), China's Unit 61398, accused of continual cyber espionage campaigns against the United States (Mandiant 2013), and the increasing sophistication in Iran's cyber warfare tactics (Aitel 2015). Traditional power dynamics are also undermined by the paradoxical idea that the most technologically advanced countries are also the most dependent on digital infrastructure and thus the most vulnerable to a crippling cyber-attack (Kolet 2001, 282). On the other hand, Lindsay (2013) argues that only the technological superpowers possess the ability to develop the most sophisticated cyber weaponry which suggests the cyber domain's asymmetric nature may be overstated.

Realism also raises the question of whether cyber capabilities give states' coercive power, referring to the capacity to induce compellence to one's will through inflicting or threatening damage upon an enemy (Schelling 1966, 1–34). There are serious doubts about the efficacy of cyber coercion, however, since the technology lacks the destructiveness of conventional military operations and is less likely to be taken seriously by the target state. Gartzke (2013, 2) highlights the limitations of internet-based warfare writing that: 'It is one thing for an opponent to idle a country's infrastructure, communications or military capabilities. It is quite another to ensure that the damage inflicted translates into a lasting shift in the balance of national capabilities or resolve.' He suggests that cyber weapons can only be effective when used simultaneously with conventional military operations. This argument has found empirical support in a statistical study on the effectiveness of different cyber offensive methods. Jensen, Valeriano, and Maness (2016) analyse data on cyber incidents between rival states and find that coercive cyber actions aimed at changing the behaviour of the target are generally ineffective compared with smaller scale disruption or espionage. These findings suggest that traditional notions of power and war do not necessarily translate well to the cyber domain, and that cyber power is not transformative of international politics.

The Cyber Offensive

The idea that attacking is cheaper, easier, more effective, and therefore a more prevalent strategy than defending features prominently in the cyber security discourse (Lieber 2014). This is based on the offense-defence balance theory which is used by defensive realists to explain why status quo powers are sometimes incentivised to go to war, postulating that when the prevailing military technology favours offensive over defensive operations, the prospects for interstate conflict increase (Quester 1977, Jervis 1978, Lynn-Jones 1995, Van Evera 1998). The offense is dominant in the international system, as Jervis (1978, 187) explains, when 'it is easier to destroy the other's army and take its territory than it is to defend one's own', and defence is dominant when 'it is easier to protect and to hold than it is to move forward, destroy, and take.'

When the advantage lies with the attackers, status quo powers are given strong incentives to increase their offensive capabilities and seek expansion or else risk being attacked themselves (Jervis 1978, 187–194). Technological factors are considered to shape the offense-defence balance in various ways. For instance, mobility enhancing technologies are said to favour the attackers, whereas technologies that increase firepower make defending more effective (Glaser and Kaufmann 1998). The theory has been used to explain the onset or absence of war in history, such as World War I, where the revolution in small arms and artillery created a widespread, albeit mistaken, belief among European leaders in the 'cult of the offensive' that encouraged them to launch pre-emptive wars or risk being attacked themselves. In reality, technology heavily favoured the defence as trench warfare demonstrated (Van Evera 1984). The theory has been thoroughly criticised, however, for its flawed logic and lack of parsimony (Davis, Finel, and Goddard 1998). More critically, Gortzak et al. (2005) demonstrate the theory's lack of empirical support as an explanation for interstate conflict. They find that neither the actual nor perceived offense-defence balance is a statistically significant predictor of war or militarised interstate disputes, thus challenging the entire enterprise.

Despite the challenges, the theory has found a resurgent popularity in the cyber security debate. The cyber offense is widely assumed to be more effective than defence due to its relative ease and cheapness, the potential damage it could inflict on society, its instantaneous nature, and because attacks need only target a single vulnerability to succeed, whereas defence involves securing entire networks and patching vulnerabilities that the defender is unaware of before they have been exploited (Lieber 2014, 100–3). Libicki (2009, 32) claims that offensive capabilities are a more cost-effective investment in that 'another dollar's worth of offense requires far more than another dollar's worth of defence to restore prior levels of security'. Going further, Saltzman (2013, 43–4) reconceptualises the offense-defence theory to fit the non-territorial nature of cyber technologies with 'versatility' and 'byte-power' replacing mobility and firepower as the key determinants of the offense dominance of cyberspace.

There are two important reasons to argue that these claims are overstated. Real-world cases can help demonstrate that, first, the utilisation of cyber weapons is not as easy or cheap as is often assumed, therefore casting doubt on one of the main determinants of the offense-defence balance, and second, that the utility of cyber weapons as a coercive tool of warfare is likely overstated, suggesting that offensive cyber operations are not necessarily advantageous.

Rather than being an easy operation, the 'Stuxnet' virus, that was developed and implemented by the United States and Israel and discovered in the networks of an Iranian nuclear power facility in 2010, was, according to experts, a complex operation that took several years to develop, costing as much as $300 million, and which likely required a human operative (Valeriano and Maness 2015, 151). The incident, which had intended to hold back Iran's enrichment of nuclear material, destroyed one fifth of the facility's centrifuges (Sanger 2012, 205). However, the rate of enrichment actually increased during this episode, highlighting the limited impact of even the most advanced of offensive cyber actions (Lindsay 2013, 391).

Similar conclusions can be drawn from the December 2015 hack of the Ukrainian power grid which caused a blackout for over 230,000 residents in Western Ukraine. The incident involved Russian hackers disabling power supplies and launching a telephone denial of service attack against customer service call centres to prevent responses to the outages. Far from being an easy operation, the logistics and months of preparation involved were considered 'highly sophisticated' (Zetter 2016). The attack was also clearly limited in its impact on the target in that power was quickly restored, due to a manual override system. These prominent incidents suggest that offensive cyber operations are neither cheap, easy, nor effective in achieving strategic victory.

In line with the predictions made by the offense-defence balance hypothesis, even if we grant that the cyber domain is offense dominant, or at least perceived to be, then it begs the question of why we haven't witnessed a greater incidence of cyber conflict. The empirical record shows, to the contrary, that between 2001 and 2011, only 20 out of 126 rival pairs of states engaged in cyber conflict which has mostly occurred at low levels of severity (Valeriano and Maness 2014, 1). The usage of cyber weapons, therefore, does not appear to be determined by the supposed offensive nature of cyber technology. Given current realities, the offense-defence balance theory is unlikely to be useful in predicting cyber conflict. What is more dangerous is if policy makers shape their policies around assumptions of offense-dominance, build-up offensive capabilities, and risk destabilising the cyber domain.

Cyber Deterrence

For realists, the acquisition of military capabilities is key to deterring aggression from other states and maintaining national security (Morgenthau 1947, 14). Deterrence aims at discouraging attacks through a demonstration of one's military capacity and willingness to respond in kind. Deterrence theory rose to prominence during the Cold War because of the threat of mutually assured destruction from nuclear weapons, and realists figure prominently in the debate arguing that nuclear weapons have a stabilising effect on international relations (Waltz 1990; Mearsheimer 1990, 19–20). Deterrence logic now appears to be influencing cyber policy. For example, in its national cyber security strategy, the US government policy is aimed at 'convincing a potential adversary that it will suffer unacceptable costs if it conducts an attack on the United States' (Department of Defense 2015), and the UK government, too, has spoken explicitly about the need to respond to cyber incidents with offensive actions (Elgot 2016).

Although it may seem an attractive option because of the perceived difficulty of defence as discussed earlier, there are several issues that undermine cyber deterrence. First, a state's ability to retaliate is not physically demonstrable due to the virtual nature of cyber weapons and the secrecy states maintain over them. Second, unlike nuclear weapons, cyber weapons do not have the same destructive capacity and so, to have a sufficient deterrent effect, would have to be used repeatedly and to great effect. This is difficult, however, because each cyber weapon is designed for a specific vulnerability which could be subsequently patched. Third, attributing the source of cyber incidents can be difficult and perpetrators often deny involvement. In such cases, therefore, a state cannot be certain of whom to respond against (Libicki 2009, 39–73). These arguments suggest that deterring aggression through cyber means is an unworkable policy in practice.

Considering the difficulties of deterrence when restricted to the cyber domain, moving towards a more inclusive idea of cross domain deterrence may offer a way forward (Gartzke and Lindsay 2014). It is also a concerning point that, while appreciating the inherent difficulties in protecting networks, governments may not be prioritising defensive measures (Rid 2013, 173; McGraw 2013, 110; Craig and Valeriano 2016b). Critical infrastructure often remains undefended, or reliant on older technology. It has been reported, for instance, that the Department of Homeland Security's EINSTEIN intrusion detection system has failed to detect 94% of the most common types of vulnerabilities (Sternstein 2016). Deterrence as a theory depends on the ability of the target state to survive a first strike, and this nuance is lost in discussions of cyber deterrence.

Another concern is the lack of discussion of the sources of discontent between entities that would lead to conflict in the first place. Given that much cyber conflict takes place between historically rival states (Valeriano and Maness 2014), often over territorial issues, perhaps working towards the settlement of outstanding issues of contention between actors ought to be given greater priority over nebulous and indemonstrable threats of retaliation.

Conclusion

As a theory mostly concerned with issues of national security and power, realism would appear to be the instinctive international relations perspective for understanding cyber conflict. Our analysis suggests that realism does remain a relevant framework for identifying important security-related issues in the cyber domain and can sometimes provide useful insights about some enduring characteristics of international relations. However, realist theories about conflict often fall substantially short in explaining the unique dynamics of cyber conflict.

In many ways, the cyber domain resembles a realist world with its anarchical nature and lack of institutional governance where states fear one another and develop their capabilities in response. Yet, it is unclear whether cyber arms races are likely to escalate into cyber conflict. Realism also raises interesting questions about cyber power, about who possesses it, and how it relates to international stability. In terms of whether cyber power will transform traditional power dynamics, the evidence suggests this is not the case. The trend we have seen thus far has been restrained from full-blown cyber war in favour of less destructive forms of cyber interactions.

The offense-defence balance is the clearest example of a realist theory being used to explain the cyber domain, but it appears empirically inaccurate in its assumptions about the cyber domain and its predictions about cyber conflict. Real-world cases of cyber conflict suggest the offense is not as easy as is often assumed and the fact that we have not seen much cyber conflict suggest the theory is misplaced. Importing the notion of deterrence from the nuclear era is furthermore ill-judged and makes little sense in the context of the reality of cyber weapons.

Prudence, a foundation of classical realism, may offer the most viable policy advice. As Machiavelli notes, the Prince 'should proceed moderately and with prudence and humanity, so that an excess of confidence may not make him incautious' (Vasquez 1995, 17). Due to the uncertainty surrounding the use of cyber technology as an offensive weapon, states should proceed with caution in the cyber domain and focus on creating resilient defences. Indeed, by refraining from outright cyber war, many states have so far remained rather prudent in their behaviour in cyberspace and this is an outcome that realist theorists would find appealing and an area for further theoretical elaboration.

Given the issues raised here, we encourage the development of new theories based on empirical observation or the deductive logics of the cyber domain rather than automatically falling back on realist theories that were developed to explain kinetic forms of warfare. With further empirical research, we can gain more precise understandings of key issues such as the impact of cyber arms races on interstate relations, the distribution of cyber capabilities among state and non-state actors, and the reasons for restraint despite the intense security competition and perceptions of an offensive advantage. More precise answers to these questions can help us formulate better policy guidance for governments.

References

Aitel, Dave. 2015. "Iran is emerging as one of the most dangerous cyber threats to the US". *Business Insider UK*, 2 December. http://uk.
businessinsider.com/iran-is-emerging-as-one-of-the-most-dangerous-cyber-threats-to-the-us-2015-12?r=US&IR=T

Arquilla, John and David Ronfeldt. 1993. "Cyberwar is Coming!". *Comparative Strategy* 12(2): 141–165.

Bumiller, Elisabeth and Thom Shanker. 2012. "Panetta Warns of Dire Threat of Cyberattack on U.S.". *The New York Times*, 11 October. http://www.nytimes.com/2012/10/12/world/panetta-warns-of-dire-threat-of-cyberattack.html

Cavelty, Myriam D. 2008. *Cyber-Security and Threat Politics: US efforts to secure the information age*. London: Routledge.

Clarke, Richard A. and Robert K. Knake. 2010. *Cyber War: The Next Threat to National Security and What to Do About It*. New York: Ecco.

Corera, Gordon. 2015. "Rapid escalation of the cyber-arms race". *BBC News*, 29 April. http://www.bbc.co.uk/news/uk-32493516

Craig, Anthony J. S. and Brandon Valeriano. 2016a. "Conceptualising Cyber Arms Races." IEEE Proceedings for CCDCOE CyberCon, 8th International Conference on Cyber Conflict: Cyber Power, 141–158.

Craig, Anthony J. S. and Brandon Valeriano. 2016b. "Reacting to Cyber Threats: Protection and Security in the Digital Era". *Global Security and Intelligence Studies* 1(2): 21–41.

Davis, James W., Bernard I. Finel, and Stacie E. Goddard. 1998. "Correspondence: Taking Offense at Offense Defense Theory". *International Security* 23(3): 179–206.

Department of Defense. 2015. "The DOD Cyber Strategy". 17 April. http://www.defense.gov/Portals/1/features/2015/0415_cyberstrategy/Final_2015_DoD_CYBER_STRATEGY_for_web.pdf

Elgot, Jessica. 2016. "UK must build cyber-attack capability, chancellor says". *The Guardian*, 1 November. https://www.theguardian.com/politics/2016/nov/01/uk-must-build-cyber-attack-capability-chancellor-says-cybersecurity

Eriksson, Johan and Giampiero Giacomello. 2006. "The Information Revolution, Security, and International Relations: (IR) Relevant Theory?". *International Political Science Review* 27(3): 221–244.

Gartzke, Erik. 2013. "The Myth of Cyberwar: Bringing War on the Internet Back Down to Earth". *International Security* 38(2): 41–73.

Gibler, Douglas M., Toby J. Rider, and Marc L. Hutchison. 2005. "Taking Arms Against a Sea of Troubles: Conventional Arms Races During Periods of Rivalry". *Journal of Peace Research* 42(2): 131–147.

Glaser, Charles L. 2004. "When Are Arms Races Dangerous? Rational versus Suboptimal Arming". *International Security* 28(4): 44–84.

Glaser, Charles L., and Chaim Kaufmann. 1998. "What is the offense-defense balance and can we measure it?". *International Security* 22(4): 44–82.

Gortzak, Yoav, Yoram Z. Haftel, and Kevin Sweeney. 2005. "Offense-Defense Theory: An Empirical Assessment". *Journal of Conflict Resolution* 49(1): 67–89.

Hansen, Lene and Helen Nissenbaum. 2009. "Digital Disaster, Cyber Security, and the Copenhagen School". *International Studies Quarterly* 53: 1155–75.

Jensen, Benjamin, Ryan C. Maness, and Brandon Valeriano. 2016. "Cyber Victory: The Efficacy of Cyber Power". Unpublished Manuscript.

Jervis, Robert. 1978. "Cooperation Under the Security Dilemma". *World Politics* 30(2): 167–214.

Kolet, Kristin S. 2001. "Asymmetric Threats to the United States". *Comparative Strategy* 20(3): 277–292.

Lord, Kristin M. and Travis Sharp. 2011. "America's Cyber Future: Security and Prosperity in the Information Age". *Center for a New American Security,* 1: 1–62. https://s3.amazonaws.com/files.cnas.org/documents/CNAS_Cyber_Volume-I_0.pdf

Lango, Hans-Inge. 2016. "Competing Academic Approaches to Cyber Security". *Conflict in Cyber Space: Theoretical, strategic and legal perspectives*, edited by Karsten Friis and Jens Ringsmose, 7–26. London: Routledge.

Libicki, Martin C. 2009. *Cyberdeterrence and Cyberwar*. Santa Monica: RAND Corporation.

Lieber, Kier. 2014. "The Offense-Defense Balance and Cyber Warfare". *Cyber Analogies*, edited by Emily O. Goldman and John Arquilla. Monterey, California: Naval Postgraduate School.

Lindsay, Jon R. 2013. "Stuxnet and the Limits of Cyber Warfare". *Security Studies* 22(3): 365–404.

Lindsay, Jon R. and Erik Gartzke. 2016. "Cross-Domain Deterrence as a Practical Problem and a Theoretical Concept". *Cross-Domain Deterrence: Strategy in an Era of Complexity*, edited by Erik Gartzke and Jon R. Lindsay. La Jolla, CA: Manuscript.

Lynn-Jones, Sean M. 1995. "Offense-Defense Theory and its Critics". *Security Studies* 4(4): 660–691.

Mandiant. 2013. "Exposing One of China's Cyber Espionage Units". 19 February. (https://www.fireeye.com/content/dam/fireeye-www/services/pdfs/mandiant-apt1-report.pdf, Accessed 06/05/2017)

McCarthy, Justin. 2016. "Americans Cite Cyberterrorism Among Top Three Threats to U.S.". *Gallup*, 10 February. http://www.gallup.com/poll/189161/americans-cite-cyberterrorism-among-top-three-threats.aspx

McGraw, Gary. 2013. "Cyber War is Inevitable (Unless We Build Security In)". *Journal of Strategic Studies* 36(1): 109–119.

Mearsheimer, John J. 1990. "Back to the Future: Instability in Europe After the Cold War". *International* Security 15(1): 5–56.

Mearsheimer, John J. 2001. *The Tragedy of Great Power Politics*. New York: W. W. Norton & Company.

Mearsheimer, John J. 2006. "Structural Realism". *International Relations Theories: Discipline and Diversity*, edited by Tim Dunne, Milja Kurki, and Steve Smith, 71–88. Oxford: Oxford University Press.

Morgenthau, Hans J. 1948. *Politics among Nations: The Struggle for Power and Peace*. New York: Alfred A. Knopf.

Mulrine, Anna. 2016. "How North Korea built up a cadre of code warriors prepared for cyberwar". *Christian Science Monitor*, 6 February. http://www. csmonitor.com/World/Passcode/2015/0206/How-North-Korea-built-up-a-cadre-of-code-warriors-prepared-for-cyberwar

Nye, Joseph S. 1990. "Soft Power". *Foreign Policy* 80: 153–171.

Nye, Joseph S. 2011. *The Future of Power*. New York: Public Affairs.

Paletta, Damien, Danny Yadron, and Jennifer Valentino-Devries. 2015. "Cyberwar Ignites a New Arms Race". *Wall Street Journal*, 11 October. http://www.wsj.com/articles/cyberwar-ignites-a-new-arms-race-1444611128

Quester, George H. 1977. *Offence and Defence in the International System*. New York: John Wiley and Sons.

Reardon, Robert, and Nazli Choucri. 2012. "The Role of Cyberspace in International Relations: A View of the Literature". Paper presented at the 2012 ISA Annual Convention, San Diego, CA. 1 April.

Richardson, Lewis F. 1960. *Arms and Insecurity: A Mathematical Study of the Causes and Origins of War*, edited by Nicolas Rashevsky and Ernesto Trucco. Pittsburgh: The Boxwood Press.

Rid, Thomas, and Peter McBurney. 2012. "Cyber-Weapons". *The RUSI Journal* 157(1): 6–13.

Rid, Thomas. 2013. *Cyber War Will Not Take Place*. London: C Hurst & Co Publishers Ltd.

Ripsman, Norrin M., Jeffrey W. Taliaferro, and Steven E. Lobell. 2016. *Neoclassical Realist Theory of International Politics*. New York: Oxford University Press.

Rosecrance, Richard, and Arthur Stein. 1993. *The Domestic Bases of Grand Strategy*. Ithaca: Cornell University Press.

Russett, Bruce and Jon ONeal. 2001. *Triangulating Peace: Democracy, Interdependence, and International Organizations*. New York: W. W. Norton & Company.

Saltzman, Ilai. 2013. "Cyber Posturing and the Offense-Defense Balance". *Contemporary Security Policy* 34: 40–63.

Sample, Susan G. 1997. "Arms Race and Dispute Escalation: Resolving the Debate". *Journal of Peace Research* 31(1): 7–22.

Sanger, David E. 2012. *Confront and Conceal: Obama's Secret Wars and Surprising Use of American Power*. New York: Random House.

Schelling, Thomas C. 1966. *Arms and Influence*. New Haven, CT: Yale University Press.

Schmidt, Brian C. 2002. "On the History and Historiography of International Relations". In *Handbook of International Relations,* edited by Walter Carlsnaes, Thomas Risse, and Beth A. Simmons, 3–22. London: Sage Publications.

Schroeder, Paul W. 1994. "Historical Reality vs. Neo-realist Theory". *International Security* 19(1): 108–148.

Senese, Paul D. and John A. Vasquez. 2008. *The Steps to War: An Empirical Study*. Princeton: Princeton University Press.

Sternstein, A. 2016. "US Homeland Security's $6B Firewall Has More Than a Few Frightening Blind Spots". *Defense One*, 29 January. (http://www.defenseone.com/technology/2016/01/us-homeland-securitys-6b-firewall-has-more-few-frightening-blind-spots/125528/?oref=DefenseOneFB, Accessed 06/06/2017)

The Economist. 2010. "War in the fifth domain: Are the mouse and keyboard the new weapons of conflict?". 1 July. (http://www.economist.com/node/16478792, accessed 06/06/2017)

Valeriano, Brandon and Ryan C. Maness. 2014. "The dynamics of cyber conflict between rival antagonists, 2001–11". *Journal of Peace Research* 51(3): 347–360.

Valeriano, Brandon and Ryan C. Maness. 2015. *Cyber War versus Cyber Realities: Cyber Conflict in the International System*. New York: Oxford University Press.

Valeriano, Brandon and Ryan C. Maness. 2016. "Cyber Spillover Conflicts: Transitions from Cyber Conflict to Conventional Foreign Policy Disputes?". *Conflict in Cyber Space: Theoretical, Strategic, and Legal Perspectives,* edited by Jens Ringsmore and Karsten Friis, 45–64. London: Routledge.

Van Evera, Stephen. 1984. "The Cult of the Offensive and the Origins of the First World War". *International Security* 9(1): 58–107.

Van Evera, Stephen. 1998. "Offense, Defense, and the Causes of War". *International Security* 22(4): 5–43.

Vasquez, John A. 1993. *The War Puzzle*. Cambridge: Cambridge University Press.

Vasquez, John A. 1995. *Classics of International Relations*. London: Pearson.

Vasquez, John. 1997. "The Realist Paradigm and Degenerative versus Progressive Research Programs: An Appraisal of Neotraditional Research on Waltz's Balancing Proposition". *The American Political Science Review* 91(4): 899–912.

Waltz, Kenneth N. 1979. *Theory of International Politics*. London: Addison-Wesley.

Waltz, Kenneth N. 1990. "Nuclear Myths and Political Realities". *American Political Science Review* 84(3): 731–745.

Zetter, Kim. 2016. "Inside the cunning, unprecedented hack of Ukraine's power grid". *Wired*. March 3. https://www.wired.com/2016/03/inside-cunning-unprecedented-hack-ukraines-power-grid/

8

Realism and Peaceful Change

ANDERS WIVEL

Realism is most often depicted as a tradition or perspective on international relations explaining war and military conflict. This is not without reason as realists have focused on war as a major or even the primary mechanism of change in international relations. Thucydides, in *The History of the Peloponnesian War,* written in the fifth century BC, and a standard reference in textbook accounts of the realist tradition, found that '[t]he growth of the power of Athens, and the alarm which this inspired in Lacedaemon, made war inevitable' (Thucydides 431 BCE, 1.23). This position is echoed in realism up until today. For instance, in his modern classic, aptly entitled *War and Change in World Politics*, Robert Gilpin asserts that 'a precondition for political change lies in a disjuncture between the existing social system and the redistribution of power towards those actors who would benefit most from a change in the system', and that change in international relations typically equals war (Gilpin 1981, 9). Likewise, John Mearsheimer, in *The Tragedy of Great Power Politics*, argues that the most war-prone regions are those characterised by unbalanced multipolarity with a potential hegemon seeking to change the established order in its favour by military means, and that the growth of China constitutes the greatest danger to world peace (Mearsheimer 2001).

This does not mean that realists are unconcerned with peace. Acting as policy advisors or foreign policy commentators, realists have often been among the most vocal critics of war. Hans Morgenthau and Kenneth Waltz, arguably the two most prominent realists in the latter half of the twentieth century, were both highly critical of US military intervention in Vietnam (Rafshoon 2001; Humphreys 2013). More recently, 'almost all realists in the United States – except for Henry Kissinger – opposed the war against Iraq' in 2003 (Mearsheimer 2005), and realists have been highly critical of the US military interventions during the Obama administration from 2009 to 2017 (Walt 2016). However, despite this concern with peace, war remains the primary mechanism for change in realist theory, and realists have been surprisingly reluctant to explore the potential for peaceful change.

This chapter seeks to remedy this shortcoming by exploring how the logic(s) of realism may help to explain peaceful change. The intention is not to test realist hypotheses on peaceful change, but rather discuss what dynamics of peaceful change we see when we look through the realist lens (cf. Smith 2007; Sterling-Folker 2006). I develop my argument in five steps. First, I define what peaceful change is when looking through realist lenses. Second, I explain why realists should be concerned about peaceful change and explain why peaceful change has until now played a marginal role in realist analyses. Third, I challenge what is typically perceived as a mission impossible in structural realism arguing that even offensive realist logic leaves room for peaceful change and may explain why peaceful change is a useful strategy for power-maximising states. Fourth, I take this argument further by exploring how increased interaction capacity has changed the power-calculus of interest maximising states, and fifth, in the last section before the conclusion, I explore how structural incentives interact with domestic politics.

What is Peaceful Change?

Realists agree with most standard definitions that peace entails the 'absence of war and other forms of overt violence' (Anderson 2004, 102). However, to the realist, 'peaceful' does not equal power free. In contrast, realists find that the prospects for peace are conditioned on the distribution of power, although they do not provide clear guidance as to which distribution will most effectively promote peace. Highly asymmetrical distributions of power such as bipolarity and unipolarity may underpin peace understood as the absence of war, because of the clarity of signals and information when there is little doubt on which actors are the strongest and there is little chance of challenging the most powerful states (Waltz 1979; Hansen 2011).[1] However, while bipolarity is highly asymmetric when we look at the great powers *vis-à-vis* the rest, it is highly symmetric when we look at the balance between the two great powers.

The balance of power, in bipolar and multipolar systems, has been viewed as a major source of peace in realist theory, because the actors in this system are expected to deter each other from attacking (Doyle 1997, 167). Within any distribution of power, states may pursue various strategies for maintaining or changing the status quo by violent or peaceful means or by seeking to 'pass the buck', i.e. getting another state to bear the costs of maintaining or changing the status quo. Realists have typically focused on violent means of change, i.e. the use or threat of military action. To the realist, peaceful change

---

[1]   For a realist discussion of the importance of systemic clarity of signals and information, see Ripsman, Taliaferro and Lobell (2016, 46–52).

entails the use of strategies of diplomatic or economic statecraft. Diplomatic strategies for peaceful change include soft balancing, where states seek to restrain the action of other states by institutional and diplomatic means, taking advantage of information asymmetry and the ability to shift between and act outside institutional settings in order to amend or change the actions of other states but stopping short of using military means (Paul 2017).[2] Economic strategies for peaceful change are fundamentally about changing the behaviour of other states through economic incentives such as trade agreements or economic sanctions (Lobell and Ripsman 2016).

What does 'change' mean in this context? Realists agree with Martin Wight that international relations is the 'realm of recurrence and repetition' (Wight 1960, 43). International anarchy and power politics will remain inescapable features of international relations, because any policy-maker who refuses to obey the self-help logic of anarchy runs the risk of endangering the security or even survival of the state he or she represents. As noted by Joseph Grieco: 'states recognise that in anarchy there is no overarching authority to prevent others from using violence, or the threat of violence, to dominate or destroy them. This is in fact the core insight of realism concerning international politics' (Grieco 1990, 38). This understanding leaves only a limited role for peaceful change as a strategy or outcome softening, but not eradicating, power politics. Thus, foreign policy decision-makers may pursue strategies of peaceful change as a prudent way of promoting change and achieving a peace in accordance with their own values and interests, but with only limited impact on transforming the international system or the nature of international relations (Gilpin 1981, 209).

War and Change: Conflating Structure with Outcome

There are two reasons why realists should be concerned with peaceful change. First, a realist focus on interstate war as the primary mechanism of change seems increasingly out of synch with the empirical record. The number of interstate wars has decreased significantly since 1946 making it one of the most profound trends in international relations in the latter half of the twentieth century and the first decades of the twenty-first century (Themnér and Wallensteen 2014). Moreover, the end of the Cold War in 1989 and the subsequent collapse of what had been one of the two dominant powers for the past 45 years, the Soviet Union, in 1991 did not trigger a great power war. The Soviet Union's successor state Russia largely accepted the single most significant loss of power by any great power without a war in the

---

[2]   See, e.g. Drezner (2013), Gruber (2000) and Thompson (2009) for discussions of these types of diplomatic strategies (although not in the specific context of peaceful change).

history of the modern state system. The loss reduced Russia to the size it had had until the successful expansion by Katharina the Great in the eighteenth century and cut off access to some of the most prosperous parts of what had previously been the Soviet Union (Hansen, Toft and Wivel 2009; Wohlforth 2002). Likewise, in Europe, the reunification of Germany in 1990 was accepted by the other states in the region even though a united Germany had been a significant source of unrest and conflict on the continent in the first half of the twentieth century. More recently, the rise of China has not resulted in military confrontation with the declining US superpower despite structural realist expectations that this will almost inevitably happen (Sørensen 2013). In essence, understanding peaceful change is important if we are to understand some of the most important trends and events in international relations over the past decades.

Second, realists should be concerned with peaceful change because they have a potentially significant contribution to make. Realists remind us of the close relationship between power and politics and look for the impact of interests even when policies are couched in the language of peace, prosperity and freedom (Mearsheimer 2001, 22–7). For this reason, realists are well positioned to provide a critical perspective on liberal and constructivist explanations on peaceful change. In addition, as I will argue below, there is nothing in the realist logic that prevents realists from making a real contribution to understanding peaceful change, and, in particular, the conditions for peaceful change. Moreover, realists are proponents of a 'practical morality' providing a middle way between 'moral perfection' and 'moral cynicism' in order to navigate – and ideally reconcile – 'what is morally desirable with what is politically possible' (Lieber 2009, 19).[3] Thus, a realist perspective on peaceful change may entail important advice for foreign policy-makers.

But if realism has potentially a lot to say about peaceful change, then why have realists told us so little? This blind spot stems from an unfortunate dichotomising of potential international realms into (existing) anarchy and (utopian) hierarchy. To be sure, a distinction between international anarchy and domestic politics is a useful and necessary assumption of realist theorising on international relations. However, the structural realist stylised account of international relations as not only a state of nature but a constant state of emergency to be contrasted with rule-governed domestic politics has important, and unnecessary, consequences for the ability of realism to

---

[3]   Lieber's discussion is explicitly focused on the contributors to *The Review of Politics*, but it is here seen as a general trait of political realism. For an attempt to formulate a general 'ethical realism' based on these pragmatic premises, see Lieven and Hulsman (2006).

comprehend peaceful change.[4] If we accept a conceptualisation of anarchy/ international politics/war and hierarchy/domestic politics/peace then the international realm is exclusively the realm of coercion and war and domestic politics the realm of persuasion and peace, and by default peaceful change becomes the (unattainable) result of legislative processes and regulation – the very antithesis of realist power politics. However, as classical realists continuously reminded us, and as neoclassical realists are increasingly aware, there is considerable variation in the clarity and severity of security threats (see e.g. Wolfers 1962; Ripsman, Taliaferro and Lobell 2016).

At the same time, domestic change is often the result of developments unrelated to government regulation (e.g. bargaining on the labour market between employers and union representatives or negotiations between producers and distributors of food over the placement of products in supermarkets). Thus, whereas the anarchic international system may lack an ultimate arbiter and legislator, even in domestic politics 'the most important changes in the structure of society and in the balance of forces within it are effected without legislative action' (Carr 1981, 194). These changes are, as observed by Carr, by themselves the result of power politics. They typically result from bargaining among parties, and they are achieved in the shadow of threats perceived to be more costly or dangerous than peacefully agreeing to change, and in that sense similar to peaceful international change often agreed in the shadow of an implicit or explicit threat of war (Carr 1981, 199). Thus, whereas structure is important for outcome in realist theory, we should not conflate structure with outcome: change by violent means and peaceful change occur in both domestic and international politics, and both may be the result of power politics.

Mission Impossible? Peaceful Change in International Anarchy

'The problem of peaceful change', writes E.H. Carr, 'is, in national politics, how to effect necessary and desirable changes without revolution, and, in international politics, how to effect such changes without war' (Carr 1981, 191–192). In domestic politics, the spread of liberal democracy and the rule of law have created mechanisms for change such as parliamentary and presidential elections and secured a regulated use of tools for change such as strikes and political protest. However, as Carr notes, 'in international

---

[4]   For an example of this understanding for world politics, see e.g. John Mearsheimer, who notes that '[s]tates [...] are fated to clash as each competes for advantage over the others. This is a tragic situation, but there is no escaping it unless the states that make up the system agree to form a world government. Such a vast transformation is hardly a realistic prospect. However, so conflict and war are bound to continue as large and enduring features of world politics' (Mearsheimer 2001, xi-xii).

politics, the question of procedure is complicated by the unorganised character of the international community' (Carr 1981, 193). The effect is fewer and less effective checks on the use of violence as a tool for change than in the domestic realm.

Students of international relations, realists in particular, typically conceptualise the unorganised character of the international realm as 'anarchy'. To structural realists, anarchy, understood as the absence of a legitimate monopoly of violence, explains the recurrence of war in international relations. As noted by Waltz, 'competition and conflict among states stem directly from the twin facts of life under conditions of anarchy: States in an anarchic order must provide for their own security, and threats or seeming threats to their security abound' (Waltz 1988, 619). The offensive realist variant of structural realism views state behaviour as a rational response to structural incentives (Mearsheimer 2001). Security seeking states will seek to accumulate power as power deters other states from attacking or dominating them in international anarchy. Power is conceptualised as latent power, composed of societal resources, most importantly population and wealth, underpinning military power, which is viewed as the final arbiter in the anarchic international system. Rational states will seek to minimise their own costs and incur costs on other states. For this reason, great powers tend to pass the buck, rather than balance, when confronted with a rising power in order to avoid spending on deterring the rising power themselves and potentially weaken rivalling states that spend the costs necessary for deterring the rising power. The most powerful state in the system is also the most secure state as power deters other states from attacking and threatening its survival (Mearsheimer 2001, 33). However, global hegemony is practically unattainable and the competition between states attempting to gain power at the expense of others is therefore endemic: 'international politics has always been a ruthless and dangerous business, and it is likely to remain that way (Mearsheimer 2001, 2).

Paradoxically, offensive realism allows us to explain why this competition for domination rarely leads to war. States, according to the theory, do not lust for war, but rationally aim to increase their power in the most cost-effective way. If they do not succeed, they risk their survival. Following this line of logic, we will expect states to prefer strategies that allow them to maximise power on the cheap over costly strategies, and accordingly to prefer peaceful change in their favour over war, which is likely to be costly and to endanger the long-term survival of the state. As predicted by the logic of the theory (but not by its main proponent John Mearsheimer), this seems to hold true if we look at the behaviour of the great powers over the past decades.

The United States and Germany have both successfully achieved hegemony peacefully but under the implicit – and sometimes explicit – threat to the economic survival of the states dominated and taking advantage of their weakness after a war or crisis. In the aftermath of the Second World War, the United States made economic aid to the war-torn European states dependent on political and economic cooperation among them in the OEEC. By combining strong support for European integrations with a US security guarantee for Western Europe and conditional economic aid, the United States succeeded in creating an '"empire" by integration' (Lundestad 1998). In the aftermath of the 2008 financial crisis, Germany (supported by a coalition of smaller EU member states) demanded a set of economic reforms and policies of Southern European EU member states, Greece in particular. If Greece would not comply with strict austerity measures, the country would be forced to leave the Economic and Monetary Union (EMU), thereby closing off lending opportunities and most likely triggering an economic collapse of the country. This was a credible threat as the Greek economy accounts for only two percent of the Eurozone economy and a collapse of the country's economy was unlikely to trigger a collapse in any other economy or the dissolution of the EMU. In effect, the crisis solidified German economic and political hegemony within the Union and support for Germany from a number of small North European countries viewing German hegemony as a bulwark against economic chaos.

Even Russia under the leadership of Vladimir Putin, often depicted as 'aggressive' by US and European commentators and policy-makers, has only resorted to violent change after multiple attempts at peaceful change in favour of Russian interests. For instance, only a few months prior to the annexation of Crimea, Russia offered Ukraine a lucrative economic deal for forgoing closer relations with the European Union including discounted energy prices and a 15 billion US dollar government loan. Thus, viewed through the offensive realist lens peaceful change may be regarded as an often used and cost-effective tool for maximising power.

Like offensive realism, the defensive realist variant of structural realism starts from an assumption of security seeking states in an anarchic international system. However, rather than power-maximising buck-passing, they predict that states tend to act as 'defensive positionalists' (Grieco 1990, 40). They guard the status quo by balancing power in order to maximise the chance of securing survival in a system without a legitimate monopoly of violence, i.e. an anarchic system (Waltz 1979, 117–23), and war is typically the result of either overreaction or miscalculation (Waltz 1979, 172–3). Based on this logic, defensive realism has a hard time explaining not only peaceful change, but change in general: if international relations are characterised by states defensively balancing any rising power then it is difficult to explain any change (Schweller 1996).

However, though left largely underdeveloped by defensive structural realists, the theory points to two important processes of peaceful change in international anarchy: competition and socialisation. Competition and socialisation constitute a transmission belt between structural effects and state behaviour (Thies 2010; Waltz 1979, 74–7). As noted by Waltz, 'if some [states] do relatively well, others will emulate them or fall by the wayside' (Waltz 1979, 118). Thus, the 'sameness' of state practices in terms of each state having its own defence forces or judicial system is explained as a gradual process of adaptation over time allowing those successfully adapting to ensure their survival. This development towards 'like units' central to structural realist thinking is reinforced by competition eliminating those states that do not compete well. Competition and socialisation may be understood as macro-processes of peaceful change, but if we are to understand how they work in practice, we need to investigate in more detail the 'process variables' or 'structural modifiers' in the international system that affect socialisation and competition.

The Power Politics of Peaceful Change: Structural Modifiers in Action

Realists do not believe that structure determines state behaviour.[5] How structure affects states is affected by processes in international anarchy that are not part of the structure, yet systemic, i.e. interconnectedness between units and the consequences of this interconnectedness that by definition are neither part of the structure of the system (anarchy, polarity), nor attributes of any unit (state) in the system.[6] One such factor is the interaction capacity of the system, i.e. the 'absolute quality of technological and societal capabilities across the system' (Buzan 1993, 79). The development of communication and transportation technologies has underpinned the development of one globalised international system and has facilitated the increase of societal capabilities including shared norms and institutions.[7] To the realist, the shared

---

[5]   Even Kenneth Waltz, the most prominent structural realist, is careful to stress that his theory cannot explain 'why state X made a certain move last Tuesday' (Waltz 1979, 121; for a discussion, see Wivel 2005). Neoclassical realists take this point further by exploring the interaction between international and domestic politics (Ripsman, Taliaferro and Lobell 2016).

[6]   For discussions of the international system from a realist perspective, see Buzan (1993), Jervis (1998), Ripsman, Taliaferro and Lobell (2016) and Snyder (1996)

[7]   Thus, we come close to what English School theorists term an international society: 'a group of states (or, more generally, a group of independent political communities) which not merely form a system, in the sense that the behaviour of each is a necessary factor in the calculations of the others, but also have established by dialogue and consent common rules and institutions for the conduct of their relations, and recognise

norms and institutions have a material base, both in the technological development making it possible and in the most powerful actors of the system promoting some norms and institutions over others.

Following this logic, we might argue that the violent change, i.e. annexation of new land if necessary by the use of military means, associated with the expansion of international society through European colonisation under the condition of low interaction capacity has today been replaced by peaceful change underpinned by high interaction capacity, leading to the creation of one global market. Viewed through the realist lens, nineteenth century colonisation and twenty-first century globalisation are both essentially a case of great powers expanding their economic base and sphere of dominance, but expansion now takes the form of peaceful change due to technological developments making peaceful change more effective than war in most cases. The high interaction capacity of the present system intensifies socialisation by speeding up market integration and thereby, at the same time, increasing competition and socialisation (Wivel 2004, 14). Therefore, one global marketplace makes competition fiercer, and it is more transparent who is winning and who is losing. Moreover, the high interaction capacity has raised the costs of warfare making security less scarce and replacing security competition with geo-economic competition as the main parameter for great power competition (Mastanduno 1999; Schweller 1999).[8]

This underpins the spread of the neoliberal practices of the US superpower and its allies and thereby provides the basis for even fiercer globalisation in the future. Although accompanied by institutions and regulations of the global marketplace, these institutions are often skewed in favour of the powerful and joined by many third world countries, not because they provide opportunity for growth, but because it is even more costly to be left outside the institutions (Gruber 2000). Thus, to realists, globalisation is at the same time power politics and peaceful change. It is characterised by 'the increasing interconnectedness of the world economy, [and] occurs within the context of the global dominance of American economic and political ideas, accompanied by the spread of American mass culture' (Wolfowitz 2000, 317).

Also, the change in interaction capacity may help us to explain the shift in state practices from hard balancing, i.e. military build-up and alliances, to soft balancing, i.e. restraining the power of other states by institutional and

---

their common interest in maintaining these arrangements' (Bull and Watson 1985, 1). For a discussion of the English School and realism, see Mearsheimer et al. (2005).

[8]   Although, in the anarchic world depicted by realists, there is no guarantee that resources accumulated by geo-economic competition will not one day be used in a geopolitical military conflict.

diplomatic means (Pape 2005; Paul 2005). Increased interaction capacity increases interdependence by increasing the number and density of relations in an international system now characterised by complex interdependence; in fact, this is often what we mean by 'globalisation' (Keohane and Nye 2000). Under these conditions, states need to be able to meet the actions of other states with a more 'flexible response' than the threat of military action. Thus, whereas the past decades have seen little evidence of hard balancing against the US unipole, realists may argue that the ASEAN Plus Three (APT) and the Regional Comprehensive Economic Partnership (RCEP) are examples of states in Asia and the Pacific seeking peaceful change by soft balancing the United States (He 2015). Even the US superpower, by far the world's strongest military power, has embarked on a similar soft strategy aiming explicitly for 'dissuasion' of potential rivals, although largely as a strategy for peacefully maintaining the status quo rather than changing it (Litwak 2010, 256–9).

Agents of Power and Peace: How Foreign Policy Decision-makers Maximise Interests through Peaceful Change

'[T]he basic task of peaceful change', writes Robert Gilpin, 'is not merely to secure peace, it is to foster change and achieve a peace that secures one's basic values. Determining how this goal is to be achieved in specific historical circumstances is the ultimate task of wise and prudent statesmanship' (Gilpin 1981, 209). Thus far, we have focused on peaceful change as change by peaceful means illustrating how the logic(s) of realism may help us to understand why even interest-maximising states in an anarchic international realm dominated by power politics may choose to pursue change by peaceful rather than violent means. However, for the individual decision-maker or government, peaceful change, like any foreign policy decision or strategy, is a complex task of navigating between structural incentives and domestic values and interests. Therefore, neoclassical realists argue that the response to structural incentives of any given state is conditioned by the clarity of the incentives. Clarity is affected by systemic process variables such as interaction capacity (as discussed in the previous section), and domestic level intervening variables such as strategic culture, the images and perceptions of foreign policy decision-makers, domestic institutions and state-society relations (Ripsman, Taliaferro and Lobell 2016).

By examining the importance and effects of these clusters of variables, neoclassical realism opens realism to a discussion of the agents of peaceful change and the interaction of international and domestic variables. For instance, we may link these insights to the democratic peace literature and hypothesise that transparent domestic institutions with checks and balances on the exercise of power – such as those found in liberal democratic states – facilitate taking the lead in peaceful change, because these institutions make it harder for state leaders to bluff and more costly not to carry out threats once domestic opinion has been mobilised (Kydd 1997; Lipson 2003). This may also help us understand why attempts at peaceful change succeed or fail. For instance, the massive restructuring of the European economic and political sphere through processes of institutionalisation and integration may be compared with the relative failure of similar projects in regions such as East Asia with comparable economic incentives but uneven democratisation. However, as realists, our analysis would not begin and end with domestic institutions. Rather, it would explore how change was affected by the very different strategies of the two most powerful states in the two regions, Germany and Japan, and how each of these states related to the interests of the United States, which pursued different strategies in the two regions (Grieco 1999).

This points to the importance of foreign policy roles. As argued by Cameron Thies, socialisation may have an important impact on state behaviour and allow us to explore the motivations and varying interests of states if we analyse them in the context of role relationships between different states in the system (Thies 2010). Understanding how and why some states take on particular foreign policy roles may be used as springboard for comparative studies on peaceful change. For instance, whereas the Scandinavian countries have a reputation for acting as norm-entrepreneurs for peaceful change (e.g. Ingebritsen 2002), they have taken on very different peace-making roles in the American world order. Sweden has played an active role in developing non-military aspects of EU security policy, Norway has actively pursued a role as international mediator in peace negotiations and Denmark has played the role of staunch military ally to the United States in Afghanistan, Iraq and elsewhere.

Conclusion

'To establish methods of peaceful change is [...] the fundamental problem of international morality and of international politics', recognised E.H. Carr in 1939 (Carr 1981, 202). This problem follows logically from the realist observation that the lack of a legitimate monopoly of power in the international realm leads to 'war's dismal recurrence through the millennia' (Waltz 1988, 620) and little restraint other than those associated with power politics on those seeking change violently. However, realists have rarely sought to tackle the issue of peaceful change explicitly. This chapter has argued that from a realist starting point, logics of peaceful change may originate in the structure of the international system (as a direct consequence of rational power-maximising states responding to the incentives of anarchy), or in processual structural modifiers (such as interaction capacity affecting processes of socialisation and competition), or in the interaction between external incentives and domestic politics (e.g. foreign policy roles and institutional design described by neoclassical realists).

Two points about the nature of peaceful change as seen through the realist lens should be noted. Depending on one's philosophical worldview and theoretical disposition, they may be seen as either caveats of the realist perspective on peaceful change or alternatively as important reminders about the need to respect the logics of necessity in international relations providing the *raison d'etre* of realism and proving its continued relevance. First, realist logics of peaceful change may help us to understand peaceful change, but not peaceful transformation, i.e. the end of power politics. The realist logics of peaceful change may bring peace but this peace is always conditioned by power. It is always a peace serving the interests of some actors and going against the interests of others. In that sense realism may be used as a critical theory of peaceful change reminding us that whenever we encounter what Carr termed 'salutary' recognitions of peaceful change, these are rarely outside the realm of power and interest but an integral part of power politics (Carr 1981, 197). However, secondly, and following logically from the first point, the discussion points to no escape from power politics. Any order and any change of order is based on power politics. In that sense, realism seems stuck as what Robert Cox termed a problem-solving theory: 'it takes the world as it finds it, with the prevailing social and power relationships and the institutions into which they are organised, as the given framework for action' (Cox 1986, 208). For these reasons, the quest for peaceful change is at the same time fundamental to the realisation of the practical morality of realists seeking to reconcile their values with the interests of accommodating to the lesser evil, and under-researched by realists blinded by the perceived state of emergency following from anarchy.

Author note: My research for this chapter began when I was a visiting fellow at the Centre for International Peace and Security Studies, McGill University. I would like to thank T.V. Paul and the editors of the book for useful comments on an earlier draft.

References

Anderson, Royce. 2004. "A definition of peace". *Peace and Conflict: Journal of Peace Psychology*, 10(2): 101–116.

Bull, Hedley and Adam Watson. 1985. "Introduction". In *The Expansion of International Society*, edited by Hedley Bull and Adam Watson, 1–9. Oxford: Oxford University Press.

Buzan, Barry. 1993. "Rethinking System and Structure". In *The Logic of Anarchy*, edited by Barry Buzan, Charles Jones and Richard Little, 19–80. New York: Columbia University Press.

Carr, E. H. 1981. *The Twenty Years' Crisis, 1919–1939: An Introduction to the Study of International Relations*. Houndmills: Macmillan.

Cox, Robert W. 1986. "Social Forces, States and World Orders: Beyond International Relations Theory". In *Neorealism and Its Critics*, edited by Robert O. Keohane, 204–254. New York: Columbia University Press.

Doyle, Michael W. 1997. *Ways of War and Peace*. New York: W. W. Norton.

Drezner, Daniel. 2013. "The Tragedy of the Global Institutional Commons". In *Back to Basics: State Power in a Contemporary World*, edited by Martha Finnemore and Judith Goldstein, 280–310. Oxford: Oxford University Press.

Gilpin, Robert. 1981. *War and Change in World Politics*. Cambridge: Cambridge University Press.

Grieco, Joseph M. 1990. *Cooperation among Nations*. Ithaca: Cornell University Press.

Grieco, Joseph M. 1999. "Realism and Regionalism: American Power and German and Japanese Institutional Strategies During and After the Cold War". In *Unipolar Politics: Realism and State Strategies after the Cold War*, edited by Ethan B. Kapstein and Michael Mastanduno, 319–53. New York: Columbia University Press.

Gruber, Lloyd. 2000. *Ruling the World*. Princeton, NJ: Princeton University Press.

Hansen, Birthe. 2011. *Unipolarity and World Politics: A Theory and its Implications*. London: Routledge.

Hansen, Birthe, Peter Toft, and Anders Wivel. 2009. *Security Strategies and American World Order: Lost Power*. London: Routledge.

He, Kai. 2015. "Contested Regional Orders and Institutional Balancing in the Asia-Pacific". *International Politics* 52(2): 208–222.

Humphreys, Adam R. C. 2013. "Waltz and the world: Neorealism as international political theory?". *International Politics* 50(6): 863–879.

Ingebritsen, Christine. 2002. "Norm Entrepreneurs: Scandinavia's Role in World Politics". *Cooperation and Conflict* 37(1): 11–23.

Jervis, Robert. 1998. *System Effects: Complexity in Political and Social Life*. Princeton: Princeton University Press.

Keohane, Robert O. and Nye, Joseph S. 2000. "Globalization: What's New? What's Not? (And So What?)". *Foreign Policy*, Spring 2000: 104–119.

Kydd, Andrew. 1997. "Sheep in Sheep's clothing: Why security seekers do not fight each other". *Security Studies* 7(1): 114–155.

Lieber, Keir A. 2009. "Introduction: The Enduring Relevance of International Political Realism". In *War, Peace, and International Political Realism*, edited by Keir A. Lieber, 1–30. Notre Dame: University of Notre Dame Press.

Lieven, Anatol and John Hulsman. 2006. *Ethical Realism*, New York: Vintage Books.

Litwak, Robert S. 2010. "The overuse of American power". In *History and Neorealism*, edited by Ernest R. May, Richard Rosecrance and Zara Steiner, 246–266. Cambridge: Cambridge University Press.

Lipson, Charles. 2003. *Reliable Partners: How Democracies Have Made a Separate Peace*. Princeton: Princeton University Press.

Lobell, Steven E. and Norrin M. Ripsman. 2016. *The Political Economy of Regional Peacemaking*. Ann Arbor: University of Michigan Press.

Lundestad, Geir. 1998. *"Empire" by Integration: The United States and European Integration 1945–1997*. Oxford: Oxford University Press.

Mastanduno, Michael. 1999. "A realist view: three images of the coming international order". In *International Order and the Future of World Politics*, edited by T.V. Paul and John A. Hall, 19–40. Cambridge: Cambridge University Press.

Mearsheimer, John J. 2001. *The Tragedy of Great Power Politics*. New York: W. W. Norton.

Mearsheimer, John J. 2005. "Hans Morgenthau and the Iraq War: realism versus. neo-conservatism". Open Democracy. Last modified 19 May. https://www.opendemocracy.net/democracy-americanpower/morgenthau_2522.jsp

Mearsheimer, John, Paul Rogers, Richard Little, Christopher Hill, Chris Brown and Ken Booth. 2005. "Roundtable: The Battle Rages On". *International Relations* 19(3): 337–360.

Pape, Robert. 2005. "Soft Balancing against the United States". *International Security* 30(1): 7–45.

Paul, T.V. 2005. "Soft Balancing in the Age of U.S. Primacy". *International Security* 30(1): 46–71.

Paul, T. V. 2017. "Recasting Statecraft: International Relations and Strategies of Peaceful Change". *International Studies Quarterly* 61(1): 1–13.

Rafshoon, Ellen Glaser. 2001. "A Realist's Moral Opposition to War: Han J. Morgenthau and Vietnam". *Peace & Change* 26(1): 55–77.

Ripsman, Norrin M., Jeffrey W. Taliaferro and Steven E. Lobell. 2016. *Neoclassical Realist Theory of International Politics*. Oxford: Oxford University Press.

Schweller, Randall L. 1996. "Neorealism's status-quo bias: What security dilemma?" *Security Studies* 5(3): 90–121.

Schweller, Randall L. 1999. "Realism and the present great power system: growth and positional conflict over scarce resources". In *Unipolar Politics: Realism and State Strategies after the Cold War*, edited by Ethan B. Kapstein and Michael Mastanduno, 26–68. New York: Columbia University Press.

Smith, Steve. 2007. "Introduction: diversity and disciplinarity in international relations theory". In *International relations theories: discipline and diversity*, edited by Tim Dunne, Milja Kurki and Steve Smith, 1–12. Oxford, UK: Oxford University Press.

Snyder, Glenn H. 1996. "Process variables in neorealist theory". *Security Studies* 5(3): 167–192.

Sterling-Folker, Jennifer (ed.). 2006. *Making Sense of International Relations Theory*. Boulder, CO: Lynne Rienner Publishers.

Sørensen, Camilla T. 2013. "Is China becoming more aggressive? A neoclassical realist analysis". *Asian Perspective* 37(3): 363–385.

Themnér, Lotta and Peter Wallensteen. 2014. "Armed conflicts, 1946–2013". *Journal of Peace Research* 51(4): 541–554.

Thies, Cameron G. 2010. "State Socialization and Structural Realism." *Security Studies* 19(4): 689–717.

Thompson, Alexander. 2009. *Channels of power: The UN Security Council and US statecraft in Iraq*. Ithaca: Cornell University Press.

Thucydides. 431 BCE. *The History of the Peloponnesian War*. Translated by Richard Crawley, The Internet Classics Archive (http://classics.mit.edu/Thucydides/pelopwar.1.first.html accessed on 30 January 2017).

Walt, Stephen M. 2016. "Obama Was Not a Realist President". Foreign Policy, 7 April.

Waltz, Kenneth N. 1979. *Theory of International Politics*. New York: McGrawHill.

Waltz, Kenneth N. 1988. "The Origins of War in Neorealist Theory". *The Journal of Interdisciplinary History* 18(4): 615–628.

Wight, Martin. 1960. "Why is there no International Theory?". *International Relations* 2(1): 35–48.

Wivel, Anders. 2004. "The Power Politics of Peace Exploring the Link between Globalization and European Integration from a Realist Perspective". *Cooperation and Conflict* 39(1): 5–25.

Wivel, Anders. 2005. "Explaining why state X made a certain move last Tuesday: the promise and limitations of realist foreign policy analysis". *Journal of International Relations and Development* 8(4): 355–380.

Wohlforth, William C. 2002. "Russia". In Strategic Asia 2002–2003: In *Asian Aftershocks*, edited by R. J. Ellings and Aaron Friedberg, 183–222. Seattle: National Bureau of Asian Research.

Wolfers, Arnold. 1962. *Discord and Collaboration*. Baltimore: The Johns Hopkins University Press.

Wolfowitz, Paul. 2000. "Statesmanship in the New Century". In *Present Dangers*, edited by Robert Kagan and William Kristol, 307–336. San Francisco: Encounter Books.

9

Realism, Small States and Neutrality

ARCHIE W. SIMPSON

Since the end of the Cold War, the policy and practice of neutrality has become unfashionable. Neutrality is an institution of non-partisanship that has been commonly practiced by many small states through the ages, ostensibly as a means to opt-out of the power politics of other states. In essence, neutrality 'is a legal condition through which a state declares non-involvement in a conflict or war, and indicates its intention to refrain from supporting or aiding either side' (Heywood 2015, 144), but it is also a political strategy. In tautological terms, neutrality means not becoming involved in wars either directly or indirectly. Yet, neutrality retains some relevance in the 21st century in three important respects: there are several small states that retain neutrality, including Ireland and Switzerland; neutrality still provides some manifestation of security; it remains an option to avoid becoming embroiled in violent conflicts. Realists generally accept that neutral states exist but, 'are unable to provide a convincing explanation for the influence of neutrality' (Austin 1998, 39). This is because the practice of neutrality falls outside mainstream realist thought relating to the role of institutions. Realists follow a number of basic assumptions about international politics involving the centrality of the state and of state sovereignty, the importance of power, the political inducement of national interests, and the need for state survival. In times of conflict then, realists believe that states should balance or bandwagon following these assumptions, but neutrality sometimes provides a third option.

In appraising realism, this chapter outlines and assesses the realist perspective on small states and neutrality. Realism has an inherent bias towards the study of Great Powers (Elman 1985; Layne 1993; Mearsheimer 2001) meaning less attention is paid to small states and to their position and status in international politics. As small states are more vulnerable to external shocks and dangers, and are less threatening to Great Powers, realists are less interested in them. For some small states, permanent neutrality is adopted as a means of achieving some level of security from outside threats. The idea of neutrality goes back to ancient times, as *The History of the Peloponnesian War* by Thucydides (Warner 1954; Crawley 2006) illustrates, but it is still practiced today by a number of small states including Austria, Ireland and Switzerland.

There are many ways to define small states (Amstrup 1976; Archer and Nugent 2002; Hey 2003; Maass 2009; Steinmetz and Wivel 2010; Archer and Bailes et al. 2014) and this means there is no scholarly agreement on what constitutes a 'small state'. This results in a variety of definitions of small states usually relating to quantifiable criteria such as geographic size, population size, economic outcomes, and military spending. However, other means of defining small states exist, including self-perception, analysis of behaviour in international relations or by a combination of factors. Importantly, smallness is a relative term in which some states can be said to be 'small' in relation to others. For example, Luxembourg is small compared to Belgium and Belgium is small compared to France, and so on. David Vital (1967) argued in favor of a two-fold means of defining small states, suggesting that those advanced, industrial states with populations of 10–15 million people or underdeveloped states with populations of 20–30 million people could be categorised as 'small states'. In Europe, most states are small, including the Benelux members, the Nordic states, the Baltic States, the island states of Europe, and others such as those in the Balkans.

This chapter will review the contemporary status of neutrality through the lens of realism and the examples of small states. The chapter will first outline the Melian Dialogue from *The History of the Peloponnesian War* by Thucydides (Warner 1954). The Melian Dialogue is a seminal piece of realist writing that has retained a resonance throughout history as it establishes many of the problems associated with neutrality. The chapter will then assess the realist position on neutrality including an outline of different types of neutrality and the four guiding principles that shape neutrality. This will be followed by a discussion concerning small neutral states during the Cold War. A number of states adopted neutrality during the Cold War for various reasons largely relating to geo-political circumstances. The contemporary position of neutrality in the post-Cold War period will be discussed which will show how unfashionable neutrality has become at the start of the 21st century.

The Melian Dialogue

The History of the Peloponnesian War by Thucydides (Warner 1954) was written around 431 BC and it is said to be 'the only acknowledged classic text in international relations' (Boucher 1998, 67). The book presents a detailed account of the ruinous war in ancient Greece between Athens and Sparta, a war that lasted for approximately 30 years from 431–404 BCE. Parallels between the Peloponnesian War and the World Wars of the early 20th century can be made because of the large scale destructive consequences of these wars. In ancient Greece, states were small city states but democratic Athens was using its maritime trade to prosper and grow which alarmed many other neighbouring city states. As Thucydides writes, 'the growth of the power of Athens and the alarm which this inspired...made war inevitable' (Crawley 2006, 24). The Peloponnesian League was created under the leadership of Sparta to curtail and counter this growth by Athens (and its allies). Kagan writes that 'the Peloponnesian War was a classic confrontation between a great land power and a great naval power' (Kagan 2009, 53). The Melian Dialogue retains its relevance in the modern world regarding the idea of neutrality for three reasons: it shows that neutrality is not a new concept and that it was recognised in the ancient world; it demonstrates that debates about war and neutrality have a timeless quality; and it also highlights that realists have always shown an interest in the institution of neutrality.

The narrative about the Peloponnesian War by Thucydides establishes the cause of the war, the political debates about the war, identifies key events and infers (many) lessons about international relations. In explaining the war, the narrative of Thucydides offers a pessimistic view of human nature and infers that structural factors in international politics play a role in warfare. Many realists reading *The History of the Peloponnesian War* interpret from this that international relations is essentially about *power politics* between sovereign states (Wight 1978, 24; Kagan 1996, 25; Boucher 1998, 68; Kolodziej 2005, 49). The text also establishes Thucydides as one of the, if not *the*, founding fathers of realism (Kolodziej 2005). Importantly, while the text is about the Peloponnesian War, there is thus much to be learned about international relations, war and strategy throughout the ages.

In the book, Thucydides explains the position of Melos, a small island that was formerly a Spartan colony. Melos adopted a position of neutrality when the war began 'and at first remained neutral and took no part in the struggle' (Crawley 2006, 336). However, Athenian generals calculated that Melos could become of strategic importance if it decided to join Sparta due to its location, and this perspective lead Athens to threaten Melos. Negotiations between the Melians and Athenians are carried out, and the Melians see occupation of

Melos as a form of slavery. The Athenians argue: 'you would have the advantage of submitting before suffering the worst, and we should gain by not destroying you' (2006, 338). The Melians ask whether 'you would not consent to our being neutral' (2006, 338), but the Athenians reject this as they see acceptance of Melos as a neutral state as a strategic vulnerability. The two sides debate the situation, each with legitimate concerns. For Melos, neutrality means trying to stay out of the war, but for Athens the slightest possibility that Melos might align with Sparta is too alarming a prospect that cannot be ignored. As Kolodziej writes, 'the Melian wish for neutrality is now viewed as a threat to Athens's security' (2005, 63). From a realist perspective, this is not about 'right' and 'wrong' but is instead about national security on both sides. The Athenians send in their army and lay siege to Melos, and while there were a few skirmishes, the superior power and size of the Athenian forces leads to an Athenian victory. The Athenians are ruthless as '[they] put to death all the grown men whom they took, and sold the women and children for slaves, and subsequently sent out five hundred colonists and inhabited the place themselves' (Crawley 2006, 343).

The Melian Dialogue exhibits many realist themes such as the security dilemma, the utility of military force, the transformative nature of warfare, and that national security is of prime concern to states (large and small). It also demonstrates that neutrality is a practice that goes back to ancient times but this is partly contingent upon the acceptance of 'larger' powers. Before the war, Melos was a trading nation that had good relations with Athens and thus its neutrality was accepted. However, the war with Sparta changed the political context making neutrality unacceptable to Athens. The small size of Melos coupled with its geographic location made it vulnerable to larger states such as Athens. The Athenian strategic logic is to eliminate a potential threat leading Thucydides to assert that 'The strong do what they can and the weak suffer what they must' (Warner 1954, 302). For many realists reading the Melian Dialogue, it is the logic of Athens as a 'great' power that is important, not the position of Melos. The inherent bias (or certainly interest) towards larger states (or 'Great Powers') is clearly demonstrated by Thucydides, though this is perhaps a natural outcome for many studying international politics. It also illustrates that neutrality is sometimes ignored, or indeed pushed aside, when the risks associated with war are interpreted by belligerents as overwhelming. Dougherty and Pfaltzgraff write that, 'to the realist, politics is not a function of ethical philosophy. Instead, political theory, is derived from political practice and historical experience' (1990, 83). With the Melian Dialogue, it is clear that the neutrality of Melos has become strategically inconvenient for Athens and so military might is used to eliminate a perceived vulnerability. This is about the practical realities of war and not about ethical considerations, and thus Melos is crushed. The 'might' over 'right' argument clearly prevailed in the case of little Melos.

Neutrality and Realism

Neutrality is a much maligned and misunderstood concept. Yet, as Goetschel writes, 'neutrality used to be an eminent component of discussions on European security: for centuries it was *the* alternative to membership in military alliances and a safety belt in the case of collective security failures' (Goetschel 1999, 115). For realists, state sovereignty and the protection of state sovereignty is of the utmost importance and has to be guarded by all possible means, which means the acquisition of power becomes an important objective, and power equates to having military capabilities. But the adoption of neutrality places various limits on foreign policy options, including the adoption of policies and practices of impartiality towards belligerents during periods of international conflict (especially war) and not becoming involved in war except in instances of self-defence. For small states, though, neutrality is a means of (further) securing their sovereignty. Neutrality also means maintaining such positions during peacetime.

Neutrality provides a politico-legal framework for states to follow that involves a level of international co-operation, recognition and acceptance by the wider international community. The Hague Conventions of 1899 and 1907 (Karsh 1988, 18; Goetschel 1999, 118–9) institutionalised the legal dynamics of neutrality setting legal bounds for neutral states to follow. This included the rights and duties of neutral states, the status of individuals from neutral states, how belligerents should act towards neutral states, and the regulation of war on the high seas. Many states from around the world were signatories to these conventions including Britain, Russia, Germany, USA, Brazil, Korea and Uruguay. A third set of conventions was planned for 1915 but the First World War broke out. For realists, such frameworks are an imposition on state sovereignty as they run counter to realist principles. States, according to realist thought, should be motivated by national interests (including national security) rather than by international practices (or institutions) like neutrality. For neo-realists, the anarchical nature of international politics is key to understanding the behaviour of states which should lead to states balancing or bandwagoning (Waltz, 1979). While realists acknowledge neutrality exists, they have some difficulty in explaining why it exists (Austin 1998, 39–41).

Neutrality is a contrivance of statecraft usually associated with small states. As realists are more concerned with larger states e.g. Great Powers and Superpowers, small states are of marginal interest unless they have a geo-strategic value or are an integral part of an international crisis or problem. As small states tend to have fewer military capabilities, they have to adopt policies and strategies designed to enhance their security as much as possible. In addition, geography can play an important role in determining whether a small state adopts neutrality. For a number of small states, such as Austria and Finland, their location in relation to others was a factor in becoming neutral (Hakovirta, 1983). Finland was a neighbour of the Soviet Union but a democratic, capitalist-based state, and so it was neutralised to appease the Soviets in 1948. Austria was occupied by the Allied powers after the Second World War for about ten years and became neutral in order to regain its sovereignty after occupation. Other states like Sweden, Switzerland and Liechtenstein were also part of this neutral bloc in the middle of Europe with Yugoslavia, in addition, becoming part of the non-aligned movement.

There are three types of neutrality plus the variant of non-alignment. Joenniemi writes that 'this wide-ranging elastic concept has been developed over several centuries, and its subjective meaning has been defined in large part by (in)security' (Joenniemi 1993, 289). *Ad hoc* or temporary neutrality is when states adopt neutrality when other states go to war. There are many examples of this throughout history, including Spanish neutrality during the Second World War or Iranian neutrality during the Gulf War of 1990–91. Realists recognise this form of neutrality as an expression of national interests and foreign policy. States that exercise neutrality on an *ad hoc* basis are not bound to adopt neutrality in future wars though they can do so. The second form of neutrality is *de jure* neutrality or neutrality by international law. There are two forms of *de jure* neutrality: 'neutralisation' meaning an international agreement has been reached which determines the neutrality of a state; and 'permanent' neutrality in which the state has voluntarily become neutral. Cases of 'neutralisation' include Austria and Finland during the Cold War; the best example of 'permanent' neutrality is Switzerland which adopted neutrality in 1815 following the Napoleonic wars. *Neutralisation* means that an international agreement has been imposed upon the neutral state, though not necessarily against its will (even though this does seem somewhat contradictory). 'Permanent' (or traditional) neutrality partly relates to the voluntary nature of adopting neutrality but also to the strict adherence to non-alignment over a substantial period of time. The third form of neutrality is *de facto* neutrality in which neutrality has been adopted without recourse to international law. Ireland and Sweden are *de facto* neutral states and follow policies of neutrality without signing international treaties; yet their neutrality is broadly accepted by the international community. The Vatican City State (or Holy See) is also officially a *de facto* neutral state, largely for religious reasons.

A variant of neutrality is 'non-alignment' which is a diluted form of neutrality that emerged during the Cold War. A number of states sought to opt-out of the politics of the Cold War including India, Sweden and Yugoslavia; they formed the 'non-aligned' movement. In essence, the non-aligned movement involved states that adopted neutrality in terms of the Cold War. That is, these states did not want to align with the Americans or the Soviets during the Cold War period. India, as a non-aligned state, was involved in three wars with Pakistan during the Cold War period illustrating that it was not neutral. While the non-alignment movement still exists, it is a largely redundant organisation now. For the most part, states adopt various forms of neutrality contingent upon their own political objectives, geographic position, and security needs.

In adopting neutrality, states are following four principles (Karsh 1988: Goetschel 1999; Walzer 2000). These four guiding principles are non-participation in wars involving others, not starting any wars, defending neutrality, and abstaining from any policies or actions that might lead to war. These principles establish certain legal and political obligations for neutral states; *de facto* neutrals also follow these obligations. Adopting such obligations applies to *all neutral* states. When a war begins involving other states, those states declaring neutrality should adopt a position of impartiality equally to all belligerent states. In a reciprocal way, belligerents are forbidden to violate the territory of neutral states or attack neutral states (Karsh 1988, 23). The second Hague Conference of 1907 on neutrality sets out the legal position of neutrality for both neutral states and belligerents at a time of war. The second principle is that neutral states should not instigate wars; as most neutral states are small states with smaller military capabilities and greater vulnerabilities, it is highly unlikely that such states would instigate a war. The third principle is to 'defend neutrality' which involves a number of factors including having high levels of predictability and credibility in being neutral during times of peace, having some military capability in order to have some means of self-defence, and abstaining from any policies or actions that might lead to war (which is the fourth principle). Vukadinovic writes that 'armed neutrality is one of the classical requirements of neutrality...neutral countries have always been expected to use *all means* at their disposal to safeguard their independence' (Vukadinovic 1989, 39). Political impartiality, diplomatic networking, consistency in being neutral, and developing some defensive military capability all play a role in establishing and maintaining credibility in being neutral. As it is small states that adopt neutrality, military capabilities are primarily defensive in nature and sometimes involve forms of conscription as in the case of Switzerland. Showing credibility in being neutral is of fundamental importance. For example, when the United Nations was created in 1945, Switzerland refused to join on the basis that its credibility as a neutral state might be jeopardised; it was not until a referendum in 2002 that Switzerland joined.

Small States, Realism and the Cold War

The Cold War divided the world for over four decades in the second half of the twentieth century. The ideological contest between Soviet communism and Western liberal democracy created a global balance of power which aligned favourably with a realist analysis of international politics. Indeed, for realists, a balance of power configuration is an inevitable and conscious feature of international politics, and for neo-realists it is an outcome of the international system (Sheehan 2005, 19). According to realists, power is a determining factor in international behaviour and self-preservation is the highest duty of any state. Moreover, small states tend to adopt balancing behaviour that maintains the international status quo; small states are not in a position to be revisionist states. For small states, there are underlying political forces, including geography, that shape their political options and establish certain limitations and constraints. For states like Austria and Finland, their proximity to the Warsaw Pact made them vulnerable particularly in the early days of the Cold War. Becoming neutral as a means of both preserving their sovereignty by appeasing the Soviets was a logical and appropriate stratagem. With neighbouring Sweden (for Finland) and Switzerland (for Austria) both being neutral, this perhaps further enhanced their own neutrality by becoming part of a neutral bloc. The adoption of neutrality when the Cold War balance of power was emerging in Europe in the 1950s also meant these states contributed to a status quo throughout much of the Cold War by becoming a geo-political buffer between West and East. The Soviets were arguably in a position in the immediate post-war period in which they could have occupied both Austria and Finland, as they did with other states like Poland, but the adoption of neutrality satisfied Soviet concerns. For the Americans and West European states, the neutral bloc provided a buffer zone between East and West during the Cold War (Hakovirta 1983, 570). Furthermore, acceptance of neutral states by both Superpowers demonstrated a mutual restraint that contributed to the overall balance of power. For neo-realists, the structure of international politics allowed these states to become neutral during the duration of the Cold War; neutrality in this sense becomes less an aberration and is explained as an outcome of structural pressures.

While Austrian and Finnish neutrality became part of the Cold War balance of power in Europe, Irish neutrality had a different genesis. Ireland had gained independence in the 1920s partly after a period of violent turmoil against the British which accelerated during the First World War. Ireland adopted neutrality partly because of domestic political reasons (there was a brief civil war in Ireland following independence) but also as a sign of pacifism following years of political violence and civil war. This neutrality was maintained throughout the Cold War period though Ireland maintained good relations with the USA and it was able to join the Common Market (now European Union) in 1973. Ireland was part of the 'big five' neutral states of Europe alongside Austria, Finland, Sweden and Switzerland, and some of the lesser known neutrals like Andorra, Cyprus, Liechtenstein, and the Vatican City.

Post-Cold War Neutrality

The Cold War provided a framework in which neutrality was a viable and sometimes useful diplomatic mechanism for maintaining the status quo. For example, the International Atomic Energy Agency (IAEA) was based in Vienna *because* of Austrian neutrality; and the UN has its European headquarters in Switzerland. However, neutrality became less relevant in the post-Cold War period. This is perhaps shown by Austrian, Finnish and Swedish membership of the European Union. During the Cold War, the EEC/EU was viewed by the Soviets as part of the Western Alliance in tandem with NATO (Tarschys 1971; Hakovirta 1983). In practical terms, this meant Austria, Finland and Sweden could not apply for membership fearing this would negate their neutrality; this applied to Swiss membership of the United Nations until 2002. With the end of the Cold War and the dissolution of the Soviet Union in 1991, neutrality was a more-or-less redundant concept in Europe. Neutrality had 'lost most of its significance' (Goetschel 1999, 122).

The enlargement of the European Union in the post-Cold War period was mirrored by NATO. Since the end of the Cold War, NATO developed a number of new structures and programmes including the establishment of the Euro-Atlantic Partnership Council and the 'Partnership for Peace' programme. Such developments were partly designed as part of a new security architecture for Europe, and partly to legitimise NATO in the post-Cold War period. The five main neutral states in Europe have joined the Euro-Atlantic Partnership Council, which would not have been possible during the Cold War. For realists, this indicates that the so-called aberration of neutrality has been seriously undermined in the post-Cold War period to the point at which it is now an irrelevant concept. Goetschel writes: 'the neutrals quickly shifted to a policy aimed at becoming as 'normal' as possible' (1999, 115).

Conclusions

During the Cold War period, neutrality was *sui generis* for a number of small states in Europe. As a political strategy it was designed to offer a form of insulation from the power politics of the Superpowers to protect the sovereignty of these small states. Neutrality set in play a number of constraints for these small states with the proviso that they would gain a greater sense of security. However, neutrality is contingent upon the acceptance of other states as shown by the case of Melos in ancient times, and by the Soviet Union during the Cold War, especially regarding Austria and Finland. For realists, neutral states can play a marginal role in the balance of power, but with the end of the Cold War there has been a lack of such a balance. Morgenthau writes, 'neutrality of the small European states is essentially a function of the balance of power' (Morgenthau 1939, 482). For small states, neutrality is motivated by national security concerns, but realists (and especially neo-realists) see neutrality as an outcome of the balance of power. Since the end of the Cold War, the world has seen a period of US hegemony (Layne, 1993) and neutrality has become less relevant. However, with the rise of China, the re-emergence of Russia and the economic emergence of others, like India and Brazil, a multi-polar balance of power is currently evolving. For realists and neo-realists, a global balance of power might mean a return to normal international politics, but it might also provide space for some small states to adopt neutrality.

References

Amstrup, Niels. 1976. "The Perennial Problem of Small States: A Survey of Research Efforts". *Cooperation and Conflict* 11(2): 163–182.

Archer, Clive and Neill Nugent. 2002. "Introduction: Small States and the European Union." *Current Politics and Economics of Europe* 11(1): 1–10.

Archer, Clive, Alison Bailes, and Anders Wivel. 2014. *Small States and International Security: Europe and Beyond*. London: Routledge

Austin, D.A. 1998. "Realism, Institutions, and Neutrality: Constraining Conflict Through the Force of Norms." *Commonwealth: A Journal of Political Science* 9: 37–56.

Baker-Fox, Annette. 1959. *The Power of Small States: Diplomacy in World War Two*. Chicago: Chicago University Press.

Boucher, David. 1998. *Political Theories of International Relations*. Oxford and New York: Oxford University Press.

Crawley, Richard. 2006. *The History of the Peloponnesian Wars*. Charleston: Bibliobazaar.

Dougherty, J. E. and R. L. Pfaltzgraff. 1990. *Contending Theories of International Relations*. New York: HarperCollins Publishers.

Elman, Miriam. 1985. "The Foreign Policies of Small States: Challenging Neorealism in Its Own Backyard." *The British Journal of Political Science* 25(2): 171–217.

Goetschel, Laurent. 1999. "Neutrality, a Really Dead Concept?". *Cooperation and Conflict* 34(2): 115–139.

Hakovirta, Harto. 1983. "The Soviet Union and the Varieties of Neutrality in Western Europe." *World Politics* 35(4): 563–585.

Hey, Joanne A.K. 2003. *Small States in World Politics*. Boulder and London: Lynne Rienner.

Heywood, Andrew. 2015. *Key Concepts in Politics and International Relations*. London and New York: Palgrave.

Joenniemi, Pertti. 1993 "Neutrality beyond the Cold War." *Review of International Studies* 19(3): 289–304.

Kagan, Donald. 1996. "Athenian strategy in the Peloponnesian War". *The Making of Strategy: Rulers, States and War*, edited by Williamson Murray, MacGregor Knox and Alvin Bernstein, 24–55. Cambridge and New York: Cambridge University Press.

Karsh, Efraim. 1998. *Neutrality and Small States*. London and New York: Routledge.

Kolodziej, Edward A. 2005. *Security and International Relations*. Cambridge and New York: Cambridge University Press.

Layne, Christopher. 1993. "The Unipolar Illusion: Why New Great Powers Will Rise". *International Security* 17(4): 5–51.

Lynn-Jones, Sean M. 2008. "Realism and Security Studies". *Contemporary Security and Strategy*, edited by Craig A. Snyder, 53-76. Basingstoke and New York: Palgrave Macmillan.

Maass, Matthias. 2009. "The Elusive Definition of the Small State". *International Politics* 46(1): 65–83.

Mearsheimer, John J. 2001. The Tragedy of Great Power Politics. New York: Norton.

Morgenthau, Hans J. 1939. "The Resurrection of Neutrality in Europe". *The American Political Science Review* 33(3): 473–486.

Williamson Murray, Knox MacGregor, and Alvin Bernstein. 2009. *The Making of Strategy: Rulers, States and War.* Cambridge and New York: Cambridge University Press.

Rickli, Jean-Marc. 2010. "Neutrality Inside and Outside the EU: A Comparison of Austrian and Swiss Security Policies After the Cold War". *Small States in Europe*, edited by Robert Steinmetz and Anders Wivel, 181–198. Farnham and Burlington: Ashgate.

Sheehan, Michael. 2005. *International Security: An Analytical Survey.* Boulder and London: Lynne Rienner.

Steinmetz, Robert and Anders Wivel. 2010. *Small States in Europe*. Farnham and Burlington: Ashgate.

Tarschys, Daniel. 1971. "Neutrality and the Common Market: the Soviet View". *Cooperation and Conflict* 6(2): 65–75.

Vital, David. 1967. *The Inequality of States*. Oxford: Clarendon Press.

Vukadinovic, Radovan. 1989. "The Various Conceptions of European Neutrality". *Between the Blocs* edited by J. Kruzel and M.H. Haltzel, 29–49. Cambridge: Woodrow Wilson International Centre for Scholars/Cambridge University Press.

Waltz, Kenneth. 1979. *Theory of International Politics*. London: McGraw-Hill Inc.

Waltzer, Michael. 2000. *Just and Unjust Wars*. New York: Basic Books.

Warner, Rex. 1954. *The History of the Peloponnesian Wars*. Harmondsworth: Penguin.

Wight, Martin. 1978. *Power Politics*. New York and London: Continuum/Royal Institute of International Affairs.

10

The Reluctant Realist: Jimmy Carter and Iran

ROBERT W. MURRAY & STEPHEN MCGLINCHEY

Reflections on Jimmy Carter's one term as US president (1977–1981) often place him as a principled idealist who fell prey to geopolitical events and gradually converted to a more strategically minded president midway through his term. The events that mark this out are usually seen as the November 1979 Iranian hostage crisis and the Soviet invasion of Afghanistan the following month. Following these events, Carter seemed to harden in his language, tone and policymaking – most visible in the creation of the Carter doctrine. Announced officially in Carter's State of the Union Address in 1980 in response to the Soviet Union's invasion of Afghanistan, the Carter Doctrine made it very clear to the Soviets and to the entire world that US foreign policy was very much dedicated to containing the Soviet Union, and that the US would use force, if necessary, to defend its interests in the Persian Gulf.

This approach by Carter was a marked departure from the initial tenets of what Carter had intended his foreign policy to be. Early in his tenure, Carter wanted to take focus away from the strategy of containment and to move American focus to issues such as human rights. Upon taking office, however, Carter realised just how difficult such a move would be, and more, that abandoning or eroding containment would threaten America's interests abroad and provide the Soviet Union with the opportunity to spread its sphere of influence into key areas of US geostrategic interest. In essence, Carter quickly understood that foreign policy could not ignore the realities of the international system, and that realism rather than idealism would have to be the driving force behind foreign policy decisions. The Carter Doctrine in many ways epitomised realism by identifying an area of American national interest and promising to effectively balance against Soviet aggression if the Soviets demonstrated an intention to expand into the region. Further, the bolstering of regional allies through economic payoffs, arms deals, and the promise of American military intervention if regional allies were threatened heralded back to the ideas originally proposed in National Security Council Report 68 (NSC-68) and the Truman Doctrine, but Carter updated both the language and context for his own time.

This chapter seeks to explore one key aspect of Carter's realism, being American relations with Iran. The decisions made during the Carter Administration regarding arms sales towards Iran more broadly reflect the balancing act that leaders must navigate in the divide between domestic and international politics. It is not enough to dismiss Carter's foreign policy as a tale of utopian beliefs in human rights becoming scattered in the midst of the Cold War. Instead, closer study of the Iran case demonstrates a foreign policy that was motivated by a realist sense of strategic necessity far more than domestic, or personal, political ideology. In this light, this chapter shows but one example that regardless of the circumstance, all leaders' decisions are limited in foreign policy-making due to the constraints posed by the anarchic structure of the international system. Regardless of personal ideology, party affiliation, or driving personal motivation, realist ideas about the role of the system in foreign policy decision making have timeless value, and Carter's sale of the Airborne Warning and Control System (AWACS) to Iran – used as an example later in this chapter – is a valid example of realism's core tenets. Together with the broader focus on Carter advanced here, the AWACS case opens up a new understanding of Carter as a president who displayed realist tendencies, albeit reluctantly, much earlier in his tenure than is typically observed. In assessing Carter's approach to Iran through a realist lens, it becomes clear that, despite an overall expectation that he would reduce arms sales, his grander ambitions for arms limitation would be doomed. Consequently, Carter's Iran policy, rather than resembling one of a liberal mind-set, came to reflect the more strategically minded policy path inherited from his predecessors.

Arming Iran: Accident or Reluctant Realism?

Iran had become America's largest arms customer long before Carter's emergence as a presidential candidate. Due to Iran's geographical location it became a focal point in US containment policy in the 1940s. It was a frontier state that stood between the Soviet Union and the oil reserves of the Persian Gulf. A US–UK coup was staged in 1953 to ensure that Iran remained governed in a way favourable to the western powers, with the Shah at the centre of affairs. Soon afterward, a pattern of economic and military aid became entrenched with Iran becoming a client state of the US. This support for the Shah's regime was enhanced by a series of arms sales in the mid

1960s as the Shah began to use his growing oil income to build beyond prior arrangements (McGlinchey 2013a, 2014). Two decades after the coup, in 1972, Richard Nixon travelled to Tehran with Henry Kissinger and agreed to unlimited and unmoderated arms sales with Iran – with the exception of nuclear weapons. This gesture, the so-called *blank cheque*, gave the Shah the freedom to buy whatever advanced US weaponry he chose, so long as he could pay for it. It was a unique arrangement for a foreign leader due to the lack of any effective domestic oversight for the arrangement in the US. It was also a test case for Nixon's reimagining of US Cold War strategy based on outsourcing the costs of Cold War containment to able allies and clients – the so-called Nixon doctrine (McGlinchey 2013b). The agreement catapulted Iranian arms purchases from approximately $150 million dollars in the late 1960s to being measured in the multi-*billions* per annum from 1972 onwards (State Department Report). Nixon's imperial style of leadership left Congress in the dark for several years on the finer details of arming Iran, something that would eventually haunt Carter as Congress sought to exercise its *advice and consent* role more effectively in later years.

The pattern Nixon set in place was cognisant of the strategic realities the US found itself in during the 1970s. The Vietnam War had shown the limits of the direct application of US military power. It had left America overstretched militarily, and also economically due to structural problems in the US economy that would fester through the 1970s. Passing the costs of US security to able allies in selected cases, such as Iran, was therefore a sound strategic decision. Nixon's successor Gerald Ford agreed and continued the multi-billion dollar arms sales pattern that Nixon had established with Iran. This cemented a path that a new president would find hard to break. As a result, Carter's general predilection towards arms control was overruled in the case of Iran, as were his human rights concerns. Both these positions were the cornerstones of Carter's election campaign, a signal that he was a different candidate. Hence, the seemingly contradictory picture of the Carter administration continuing a high profile arms relationship with the Shah can be accounted for due to Carter's willingness to overrule his principles in the face of a policy that had become deeply entrenched.

The idealism of Carter's campaign promises regarding foreign policy failed to take into account the reality of the international environment in which the US was operating, and more, the constraints placed on American foreign policy options by a bipolar international system. Given the well-entrenched strategy of containment throughout US foreign policy preceding Carter, it was highly unlikely to assume or believe he would, or even could, depart from the fundamental realisation reached by his predecessors that containment would remain America's primary national interest in a bipolar conflict. As Hans Morgenthau notes:

A realist theory of international politics will also avoid the other popular fallacy of equating the foreign policies of a statesman with his philosophic or political sympathies, and of deducing the former from the latter. Statesmen, especially under contemporary conditions, may well make a habit of presenting their foreign policies in terms of their philosophic and political sympathies in order to gain popular support for them. Yet they will distinguish with Lincoln between their '*official* duty,' which is to think and act in terms of the national interest, and their '*personal* wish,' which is to see their own moral values and political principles realised throughout the world. (Morgenthau 2006, 6)

In a more general sense, much has been said about the nature of Carter's foreign policy behaviour, and its failure both in terms of achieving objectives the president himself valued, such as human rights, and its overall ineffectiveness. Sometimes characterised as a liberal in the midst of a very realist Cold War, reflection actually tells a different story. Carter's foreign policy was very much built on the realist assumptions of his predecessors, whether it was intentional or not. Selling vast quantities of advanced arms to Iran is only one example of a foreign policy developed on assumptions of American self-interest and containment, rather than the rhetorical values of human rights and détente espoused by Carter during his presidency. The Carter era of foreign policy was supposed to be different, or at least that was what Carter wanted to believe. What became evident during the Carter years was the difficulty he would have in trying to promote an international policy package that mirrored his personal liberal beliefs during the constraints of the Cold War. Paul Kennedy summarises this notion by arguing:

Imbued with the most credible of Gladstonian and Wilsonian beliefs about the need to create a 'fairer' global order, Carter breezily entered an international system in which many of the other actors (especially in the world's 'trouble spots') had no intention of conducting their policies according to Judeo-Christian principles ... For all its worthy intentions, however, the Carter government foundered upon the rock of a complex world which seemed increasingly unwilling to abide by American advice, and upon its own inconsistencies of policy. (Kennedy 1987, 409–410)

To put it another way: due to the structural constraints of the Cold War, Carter 'came in like a lamb and went out like a lion' (see Lebow and Stein 1993; Aronoff 2006).

The arms trade was a particularly sensitive area for US policy during the Carter era and the administration's approach to arms, and its juxtaposition to other normative issues, are a key aspect of Carter's policy failure. As Gaddis stresses:

> The difficulty here was that Carter never related his moral and domestic political commitment to human rights to his geopolitical and (given the alternative) humane commitment to arms control. (Gaddis 1982, 348)

As such, Carter's policy towards Iran during the final phase of the Shah's rule has been referred to as his 'most glaring and costly [foreign policy] inconsistency' (LaFeber 1985, 288). This is best encapsulated in the New Year's Eve toast Carter delivered in 1977 in Tehran in which he toasted the Shah for turning Iran into an 'island of stability' and for deserving 'the respect and the admiration and love which your people give to you' (Carter 1977). It was a fateful moment for Carter as one year later the Shah was forced to flee his own country, and Iran quickly turned into a revisionist, and regionally destabilising, force. The lack of translation from domestic attitudes to the international realm is certainly not unique to the Carter Administration. All national leaders are forced to make decisions and make policy in a system that often provides little opportunity for novelty or significant change. The strategic environment in which Carter was making decisions was not very different at all from his predecessors'. It is certainly easy to claim that changes were necessary in campaign rhetoric but the issue remains that presidents have a limited ability to radically alter foreign policy, especially considering that the US was one of two superpowers dominating a bipolar international system. Like all national leaders, Carter was constrained by the Cold War balance of power that was successful in preventing the outbreak of major war between the two superpowers.

For many years, the Carter arms trading policy was a topic of insult and the go-to case for successive administrations in cautionary tales about arms sales. The Reagan administration was quick to start the effort to paint Carter as naively ideal-based on its own desire for a more liberal arms sales policy. In a 1981 address to the Aerospace Industries Association, Undersecretary of State for Security Assistance James Buckley argued that Carter's policy 'substituted theology for a healthy sense of self-preservation' (Hartung 1993, 58). What is most interesting about the vilification of Carter's policy is that arms sales were actually not restrained in any large-scale manner, and in the case of Iran, actually increased to record levels during Carter's presidency. Even as the Shah entered his final days in mid-1978, another multi-billion dollar arms deal was being tabled with Iran – and the Cold War was once again growing hotter, creating a need for increased US defence spending. In addition, a major facet of Carter's Camp David accords between Egypt and Israel was a multi-billion-dollar package of arms sales to both nations (and to Saudi Arabia) which Carter advanced to make each nation feel more secure and thereby more inclined to sign on to his peace plans. In short, despite rumours to the contrary, Carter was not shy of selling arms.

The key to understanding why Carter was so vested in selling arms to Iran is found in American perceptions of regional and international balances of power. At the international level, Carter and his advisers knew they needed to maintain Iran as a strong ally in a tumultuous region where the US had few other reliable allies of note. The regional dynamics were naturally a part of the US' larger view of the international balance of power, where the Soviets and Americans did their best to establish and maintain respective spheres of influences. With both Israel and Iran as militarily strong allies in the region, and Saudi Arabia as a powerful economic ally, the Americans felt secure knowing they had strategic assets in the region. There was also a perception that the US had a responsibility to promote democratic values, and the Shah appeared willing to at least appease the US when it made demands regarding the Shah's actions (Moens 1991, 221). Going back to the early 1960s, the Shah had established a series of domestic reforms to overcome growing questions in Washington over the validity of his autocracy. When that proved successful in winning the support of the liberal-minded Kennedy administration, despite it being no more than a token gesture in reality, the Shah became confident that he could rule largely as he saw fit and maintain his autocratic style of governance (McGlinchey 2014, 22–38). It was reassuring to the ego of certain liberal minded presidents – such as Kennedy and Carter – when the Shah appeared to make gestures towards liberalisation and reform. It made the realisation more palatable that it was more important than anything else that Iran remained pro-Western and an instrument of containment via its advanced military. The Shah, with all his faults, was the best way to ensure that – and that is why he endured through eight US presidencies.

The AWACS Sale and Carter's Realism

The Airborne Warning and Control System (AWACS) was a modified Boeing 707 jet that served as a high altitude airborne command centre. The system did not carry weapons and was outwardly defensive, allowing for the monitoring and location of enemy stationing and battlefield movements, both ground and airborne. Yet, implicitly (and simultaneously) it enabled the offensive coordination of the user's forces. For example, Iran could use the system to direct a squadron of fighter jets to an attack target. The AWACS was the most advanced system of its kind available at the time and was a generational leap in terms of technology when compared with rival systems.

Despite placing arms sales on hold in the first half of 1977 pending the launch of a wholesale arms policy review, Carter decided to sell Iran a fleet of AWACS in May. In allowing the sale, Carter was riding roughshod over two key pillars of his arms policy rethink which were subsequently outlined in Presidential Directive 13 (PD-13) (1977). Firstly, one of the central controls introduced in PD-13 was the decision not to introduce paradigm changing military technology into a region, thereby setting the precedent for arms escalation. The AWACS sale clearly violated this principle. Secondly, the heart of PD-13 was the establishment of a progressively lowering annual arms ceiling. To retain flexibility, NATO nations, plus Japan, Australia, and New Zealand were exempted due to existing US treaty obligations. PD-13 also excluded Israel, albeit abstrusely, but Iran was conspicuous via its absence from the policy paper as America's largest arms customer. Despite this, Cyrus Vance, Carter's Secretary of State, privately reassured Iran that it would also be exempted from PD-13. This led to arguments and frustration within the administration. NSC Staffer Leslie Denend summed it up in a memorandum to Carter's National Security Adviser, Zbigniew Brzezinski, as follows:

> Though this may seem like a good way to ease the Shah's disapproval of our policy, it seems to me shortsighted in the extreme. Either we mean what Vance has said, in which case we are never going to decrease arms transfers...or else we don't mean it. (Memorandum for Brzezinski from 'Global Issues' 1977)

What these points highlight is the extent of the realist attitudes embedded at the upper end of the Carter administration – and how early in the administration that foreign policy realism had set in. Whilst the staffer levels were getting their collective heads around the new arms regime and working hard to establish the policy momentum for PD-13, Vance - and as it would later turn out Carter and Brzezinski - were already introducing fluidity into the process as the structural constraints of the Cold War pressed upon them. This begged the question of why Carter bothered to add the specific countries listed in PD-13 as exceptions when he intended to exempt more nations on an ad-hoc basis, such as Iran. The language and attitude towards PD-13 and the exemption of states such as Iran again drove home the fundamental idea of conflict within the Carter Administration about arms sales and foreign policy decisions more broadly. Regardless of what PD-13 said, Carter was fully aware of the fact that the US would be forced to break his own directive to achieve the regional goals in the Persian Gulf to protect American interests.

When Carter approved the sale of the AWACS to Iran he not only went against the spirit and the letter of his own arms control doctrine, he also found himself acting as an advocate for a foreign leader against a hostile Congress. Congress blocked the sale on concerns of the technology falling into the hands of the Soviets and of the aircraft being too advanced for Iranian crews to operate. Iran was still a developing nation and was suffering from underinvestment in infrastructure and education, thanks to the Shah's preference for military expenditure. However, Carter successfully resubmitted the deal after an intense lobbying effort. The episode placed Carter in strange waters considering the anti-arms rhetoric of his 1976 campaign. Few would have expected Carter and Congress at this time to fall on opposing sides of an arms issue. Yet, the AWACS issue was the first in what would become a series of battles Carter fought with Congress over significant arms sales to a range of Middle Eastern nations. After less than one year in office, the new President had come to appreciate the value, and often the strategic necessity, of arms sales as tools of US policymaking.

Much like his predecessors, Carter used the power of the executive to manoeuvre successfully around Congressional roadblocks. However, the AWACS affair exposed a climate of doubt over US relations with Iran, and did so in a very public setting on Capitol Hill as the AWACS hearings played out. That ambiguity seriously threatened US relations with Iran, and most probably contributed to the Shah's decline by exposing cracks in his armour and allowing domestic opposition groups to gain traction. In addition, Carter subjected himself to an ordeal that indicated strongly that his team approach – which had been engineered to re-establish administrative diversity in decision-making – could be inefficient and burdensome. This can be best seen by members of Carter's own administration, principally CIA Director Stansfield Turner, expressing doubts in private testimony to Congress over the sale, giving Congress more ammunition to initially oppose it. Following the AWACS episode, Carter gradually dissolved his team approach in favour of one reminiscent of the Nixon/Ford system where decision making was ever more controlled from within the White House. This eventually allowed the strategically minded Brzezinski to reorient the administration towards a more traditional East/West mind-set that fitted with the realist bipolar view of the Cold War. While scholars recognise this shift, the AWACS case shows that Carter was already displaying a reluctant realism mere months into his tenure, as he assumed office and fully recognised the challenge of making foreign policy decisions in the bipolar context of the Cold War.

Focusing on Carter specifically, he cited a diary entry in his memoirs from 31

July 1977 where he noted apathetically (as the AWACS sale had been initially rejected by Congress) that he did not care whether or not the Shah bought the AWACS. He added that the Shah was welcome to pursue alternative systems that he was considering (Carter 1982, 435). If such a sale occurred, those alternatives would not contravene PD-13's controls, as they were *not* paradigm changing systems. Carter's curious reflection, when examining the reality of the intense administration scramble to push the AWACS sale through the summer of 1977 is therefore contradictory and outwardly confusing. What can be said for sure is that Carter's professions to Congress, to the Shah, and to his cabinet were quite the opposite from the position noted in his diary. The fact that Carter chose that one diary entry to carve his own history of the AWACS affair may be attributed to the proximity of the Iranian revolution at the time of writing and Carter's desire to give the appearance that he had maintained objectivity in his dealings with the Shah. However, the historical record shows this account to be less than accurate and perhaps highlights Carter's own unease with the choices he had to reluctantly make, given the constraints facing him in this case. Further adding to the discrepancies found in Carter's personal account, he prefaced the decision to approve the AWACS sale in the following way:

> I was attempting to reduce the sale of offensive weapons throughout the world, but it was not possible to make excessively abrupt changes in current practices, because of the contracts already in existence. (Carter 1982, 435)

This statement is interesting in two ways: Firstly, he does not refer to the AWACS as a defensive weapon. Yet, this was a central defence of the sale to Congress despite the spurious nature of that claim. Presumably this had become a frail position to remain insistent on. Secondly, there were no contracts in existence in any sense for an Iranian purchase of the AWACS prior to Carter's offer in mid-1977. The AWACS was not ready for sale until 1977.

With these points in mind, Carter's recollection of the AWACS affair is strange, and perhaps even uncharacteristic of a figure who is almost universally admired for his honesty and humanity. Explaining the contradiction goes to the heart of the quandary Carter found himself in with Iran – where the wider needs of American security placed him at odds with his personal preferences, thus channelling Max Weber's famous observation that 'Interests (material and ideal), not ideas, dominate directly the actions of men' (Weber 1926, 347).

Conclusion

By maintaining, and expanding, the arms relationship with the Shah as witnessed most explicitly in the AWACS example, Carter's experience exemplifies the lack of alternatives that existed for US regional policy in the Persian Gulf in the late 1970s. More broadly, it also displays the limitations posed by the international system on national leaders in foreign policy making. Upon taking office, Carter's inexperience and lack of knowledge in foreign policy making quickly became evident. Carter's seemingly 'absolute' commitment to human rights and arms control created an inconsistent and often ineffective foreign policy agenda. The case of arming Iran presents the earliest evidence of that inconsistency as Carter not only ignored the Shah's less than commendable human rights record, but also bolstered the selling of arms to Iran in both quantitative and qualitative measures. The AWACS was only one part of a package of arms sales in 1977 that amounted to a total higher than in any year prior. Taken strictly historically, it is difficult to explain why an arms control and human rights idealist sold a dictator with a proclivity for torturing his political opponents billions of dollars' worth of sophisticated arms. And, why he did so mere months into his presidency when presumably his ideals would have been at their most potent. Yet, this result becomes easier to explain through a realist lens by examining the strategic environment in which Carter was making decisions and the perceptions of Iran's essential role as a regional ally in the broader context of the Cold War and the overarching goals of the Carter Doctrine.

Carter's reluctant realism, and his pragmatism towards Iran, speaks volumes about how he came to understand regional stability and security once in office. Carter was content to openly admonish regimes in Brazil, Argentina and Chile for their rights records and to reduce aid to those states in an effort to compel better behaviour on human rights protection. But, when push came to shove with more valuable allies, the 'absoluteness' of Carter's human rights agenda quickly became fickle. In the case of Iran, the cause of human rights ranked lower than a strong ally in a tumultuous region, and thus Carter did what he could to maintain the pattern of relations with the Shah in the hopes of ensuring the continuation of a strong sphere of influence in the region. Carter's approach toward Iran, exemplified by the AWACS sale, demonstrates that he ultimately became more concerned with perpetuating the strategy of containment than following through on his liberal tendencies. The fact that it took only months in office for Carter to make that transition from a principled liberal to a reluctant realist is testament to the binding that the Cold War, and the structural constraints of bipolarity, placed on US presidents and foreign policy making more generally.

References

Aronoff, Yael S. 2006. 'In Like a Lamb, Out Like a Lion: The Political Conversion of Jimmy Carter', *Political Science Quarterly* vol. 121, no. 3, pp. 425–449.

Carter, Jimmy. 1977. 'Tehran, Iran Toasts of the President and the Shah at a State Dinner', The American Presidency Project, 31 December. (http://www.presidency.ucsb.edu/ws/?pid=7080 accessed 22 July 2017).

Carter, Jimmy. 1982. *Keeping Faith: Memoirs of a President*, Collins, London.

Gaddis, John Lewis. 1982. *Strategies of Containment*, Oxford University Press, Oxford.

Hartung, William. 1993. 'Why Sell Arms? Lessons from the Carter Years', *World Policy Journal* vol. 10, no. 1, pp. 57–64.

Kennedy, Paul. 1987. *The Rise and Fall of the Great Powers,* Random House, New York. 409–410.

LaFeber, Walter. 1985. *America, Russia and the Cold War*, Alfred A. Knopf, New York.

Lebow, Richard Ned & Stein, Janice Gross. 1993. 'Afghanistan, Carter, and Foreign Policy Change: The Limits of Cognitive Models', in Dan Caldwell and Timothy J. McKeown, (eds), *Diplomacy, Force and Leadership: Essays in Honor of Alexander L. George,* pp. 95–127, Westview Press, Boulder.

McGlinchey, Stephen. 2013a. 'Lyndon B. Johnson and Arms Credit Sales to Iran 1964–1968', *Middle East Journal* vol. 67: 2.

McGlinchey, Stephen. 2013b. 'Richard Nixon's Road to Tehran: The Making of the U.S.–Iran Arms Agreement of May 1972', *Diplomatic History*, 37: 4.

McGlinchey, Stephen. 2014. *US Arms Policies Towards the Shah's Iran*, Routledge, London.

Memorandum for Brzezinski from 'Global Issues' 1977. Jimmy Carter Library, 31 May. RAC: NLC-28-36-2-25-3.

Moens, Alexander. 1991. 'President Carter's Advisers and the Fall of the Shah', *Political Science Quarterly* vol. 106, no. 2, pp. 211–237.

Morgenthau, Hans 2006. *Politics Among Nations: The Struggle for Power and Peace,* 7th edn, McGraw-Hill, New York.

Presidential Directive 13 1977. 13 May. (http://www.fas.org/irp/offdocs/pd/index.html accessed 22 August 2017).

State Department Report Section II:B, 'The U.S.-Iranian Military Relationship, 1941–1979'. The Digital National Security Archive: IR03558.

Weber, Max. 1926. *Max Weber,* JCB Mohr, Tubingen.

11

Realism: Human Rights Foe?

KOLDO CASLA

This chapter appraises Realism from a human rights perspective. The first section introduces the conventional view according to which realism, with its focus on the state, material power and international anarchy, would dismiss the idea that human rights could matter at all in global politics. The second section provides an alternative perspective. There are at least three ways in which human rights can survive and indeed flourish in a world guided by classical realist parameters. I contend, first, that realism creates the space for a political critique of international law, which helps us understand the political reasons why certain claims get framed in the language of human rights law. Secondly, realism advises restraint in the use of military force, leading potentially to better human rights outcomes. Finally, realism can also allow us to theorise about a certain idea of order guided by international rules defined by states themselves.

Common Wisdom: Realism vs. Human Rights

Realism attempts to explain the satisfaction of predetermined national interests in an anarchic world based on the autonomy of politics and from a consequentialist ethical perspective. To put it another way, for realists the state has a unitary character, politics and ethics belong to different realms, and whether an act is right or wrong depends on the result of the act itself. Understood as such, realism is frequently perceived as hardly compatible with a genuine moral commitment to normative positions as those reflected in the idea of human rights.

In general, realists are strongly sceptical about international law (Morgenthau 1940; Krasner 2002), and about the international proclamation of one 'moral code' over potentially conflicting others (Morgenthau 1948). In their view, it is unwise to judge other states' actions from a moral perspective (Morgenthau

1979; Kennan 1985). States would be reluctant to accuse each other of human rights violations because they could be accused of the same thing in reciprocity, and their sovereignty would be undermined as a result (Krasner 1993, 164).

For realists, normative values and international regimes do not have power in themselves. The proclamation of human rights lacks analytical or explanatory value to account for state action. Hence, international human rights law (IHRL) does not deserve much attention. After all, IHRL is an international regime made of normative values. An international regime matters only insofar as it reflects the pre-existing 'distribution of power in the world' (Mearsheimer 1994/95, 7), and norms get subsumed 'in the material structure of the international system' (Mearsheimer 1995, 91). In other words, for realists, either the international human rights regime does not make a difference, so states will not be really bothered about it; or it does make a difference, but only as one more tool at the hands of the strong to impose their hegemonic power over the weak.

Realism is present among legal scholars. For legal realists, the proclamation of human rights in international law has very little connection with the actual improvement of human rights around the world, which has more to do with more interdependent trade relations and with the end of the Cold War. It is true that liberal democracies keep drafting, signing and ratifying human rights treaties, but in their opinion, this is only because they can do so at a very little cost, and the opposite would make them look like ugly outliers, since most other countries would not disembark from the international human rights regime (Goldsmith and Posner 2005, ch. 4; Posner 2014).

Realist scepticism towards the international proclamation of human rights has also reached the shores of scholars sympathetic to the idea of human rights, for whom realism would not have much to offer. For Michael Freeman (2002, 131), for example, 'realism can explain the neglect of human rights by states, but it can explain neither the introduction nor the increasing influence of human rights in international relations'. And Landman (2006, 44) writes that under realism states only allow human rights norms to emerge and develop 'to gain short-term benefit and raise international legitimacy while counting on weak sanctions and largely unenforceable legal obligations'.

With sporadic exceptions (like Schulz 2001 and Mahanty 2013), for most human rights academics and practitioners realism remains anathema and realists are seen as intellectual adversaries.

An Alternative View: Three Ways in Which Human Rights Could Engage with Realism

The narrative above remains the general view about realist thinking on human rights in global politics. This view is very much spread within and beyond realism. Yet, I believe an alternative realist reading of human rights is possible, particularly within the more classical and pre-Waltzian realism (before the 1970s), less constrained by the international structure and more interested in counter-arguing what was seen as reckless idealism.

The dialogue is not only possible with authors long gone, like E. H. Carr, who adopted an ambivalent position about the marriage between ideals and power: 'The characteristic vice of the utopian is naivety; of the realist, sterility' (Carr 2001, 12). Well-known contemporary realists have also made the case, albeit feebly, to let human rights into the equation of hard politics. From the United States, both John Mearsheimer (2014) and Stephen Walt (2016) have sustained that abuses committed by American forces abroad pose a serious risk to national security, and that the best strategy to promote democracy and human rights abroad is to do a better job at protecting them at home.

Realism and human rights stem from very different starting points, but they do not necessarily speak untranslatable languages. Their respective positions and agendas are not intrinsically irreconcilable. The next paragraphs will give examples in three areas where human rights analysis and advocacy could benefit from some realist thinking.

Unravelling the Politics behind International Law

Liberals assume that the legal system regulates behaviour within the political system as a whole. This premise is not shared by one of the most influential legal realists of the 20th century, Carl Schmitt. Realism reminds us that the legal and the political spheres do not match inside out.

Without a doubt, Schmitt's anti-Semitism and proactive support of the Nazi regime make him an unlikely reference in any paper on human rights. Notwithstanding the foregoing, Schmitt's representation of sovereignty as the power to decide over the confines of the rule and the exception is particularly enlightening to understand the retrogression of human rights during the so-called War on Terror (see Agamben 2005). At the very least, Schmitt should be read by human rights defenders to get a grip of the discourse that rapidly spread throughout Western countries after September 2001. This discourse is still very vivid today, and within it some have justified the use of torture against presumed *terrorists*, advocated the restriction of the freedom of movement of foreigners, and came up with a new category of fighter, the so-called *enemy combatant*, to whom international humanitarian law would not apply. The underlying idea, Schmitt taught us, is that society's enemies should not enjoy the rights and benefits society bestowed upon itself. The enemy manages to get into the political sphere but remains outside the legal one.

Schmitt denounced the alleged depoliticisation of liberalism, which pretends that morality is not a debatable issue and proclaims supposedly superior universal values applicable at all times and everywhere. Echoing the 19th century French anarchist Pierre-Joseph Proudhon, Schmitt famously warned that 'whoever invokes humanity wants to cheat' (2007, 54). One must think critically about the political reasons why certain ideas manage to resonate in international law, while others do not. In other words, legal realism invites us to explore the politics behind international law.

The Finnish legal scholar Martti Koskenniemi (2005) offers interesting insight on this. For him, international law in general, and IHRL in particular, is a double-edged sword that serves two opposite purposes at once, 'from Apology to Utopia', as the title of his book goes. On the one hand, international law is based on states' will and has the virtue of concreteness, but when it is too closely related to actual state practice, and fails to create new obligations for states, it becomes 'apologetic' of existing power, providing an excuse or a justification for it. On the other hand, international law constitutes an ideal or a plurality of ideals of state behaviour, and it can assert the autonomous normative power of the law; its potential vice, however, is that it risks being 'unreal' if it remains too disconnected from actual practice.

Extracting the meaning of human rights from international law is therefore an exercise of 'hegemonic contestation', where international actors, including state officials, publicists, international NGOs, etc., 'routinely challenge each other by invoking legal rules and principles on which they have projected meanings that support their preferences and counteract those of their opponents' (2004, 199). Koskenniemi chooses the word 'hegemony' in its Gramscian sense to refer to the predominance that requires force as much as consent and is the result of an ideological battle to set a moral direction.

Nevertheless, institutions necessarily confine the contestation. One must beware that from the very moment human rights get institutionalised, they are subject to the constraining effects of international law, where states are still the main gatekeepers. As long as international law remains the law states agree upon (apart from the interpretation, over which they do not have full control), it will be by definition limited in terms of emancipatory potential for the powerless and right holders at large. This is what Stammers (2009) refers to as the 'paradox of institutionalisation', or what Koskenniemi calls the 'colonisation of political culture by a technocratic language' (1999, 99).

The reflective exploration of the politics and the hegemonic contestation behind international law can shed light on the international legal distinction between civil and political rights (CPR: freedom of expression, right not to be subjected to torture, fair trial, etc.) on the one hand, and economic, social and cultural rights (ESCR: right to housing, right to health, right to education, etc.) on the other. While both sets of rights are recognised in international law, the fulfilment of ESCR is meant to be achieved 'progressively' depending on 'available resources', in the language of Article 2(1) of the 1966 International Covenant on Economic, Social and Cultural Rights. No such strings are attached to the International Covenant on Civil and Political Rights, adopted the very same day.

Albeit imperfect, a number of mechanisms have existed for decades to monitor compliance with CPR on individual cases both at the global and regional levels. However, individual complaint mechanisms on ESCR are newer and more inexperienced: the UN Committee dealing with ESCR issued its first decision in summer 2015, while the one on CPR examined the first cases in the late 1970s. They are also weaker: the European Court of Human Rights bests the European Committee of Social Rights in budget, number of cases heard per year, level of compliance by states, and pretty much any other possible variable. The types of violations examined are also more limited: among ESCR, the Inter-American Court of Human Rights can only know of violations of union rights and the right to education, while its mandate is not constrained in relation to CPR.

That said, international law could also be counterproductive for social justice. On the one hand, international law is meant to have universal appeal and enjoys the good standing of governmental level commitment. On the other hand, some advocates may not feel entirely comfortable with the potential trade-offs of working for material equality, fair taxation and collective bargaining within the confines of international law. Campaigns may lose out if they depend too much on international treaties drafted and negotiated by powerful elites, court rulings concerning individuals and perhaps even isolated cases, and well-intentioned reports by unaccountable UN experts published in Geneva or New York. The revolutionary strength of these tools is considerably limited, and they are unlikely to energise individuals and communities left out from an unfair distribution of global resources (find an insightful debate on this in the volume edited by Lettinga and van Troost 2015). When drawing their strategic priorities, social justice advocates may prefer to stand behind a radically leftist candidate than to spend their resources on policy papers about the legal meaning of Article 2(1) of the International Covenant on Economic, Social and Cultural Rights.

ESCR remain second-class rights in international law, and there are not theoretically compelling reasons to explain it. The reasons have to do with the Cold War context in which IHRL emerged, but also with the fact that most Northern human rights NGOs only started to work on issues related to ESCR in the 21st century. In other words, the reasons are political. Human rights analysts could use some realism to unravel the politics behind the different form of institutionalisation of ESCR and CPR in international law, but also to reconsider the pitfalls of IHRL-based advocacy for social justice.

Prudence Could Make War Less Likely

Realists see states as functionally equal. For them, states' relative power vis-à-vis each other does not depend on their role in the system, but on their economic weight and military strength. Taking functional equality as a given, realists are particularly interested in the balance of power. Realism is static, prone to the status quo, suspicious of change. In one word: realism is prudent.

As noted by Donnelly (2008, 157, 159), who is not a realist,

> Realism is best read as a cautionary ethic of political prudence rooted in a narrow yet insightful vision of international politics. [...] A defensible realist ethic is perhaps best seen as a warning against the inappropriate application of moral standards to international political action.

Considering its prudence in international affairs, realism may prove most valuable in making sure that we exhaust all available resources before going to war. And this matters because nowhere are human rights more at peril than on the battlefield. Realists would not use moral arguments to oppose military interventions, but they can become tactical allies on a case-by-case basis. For example, Morgenthau (1965) was an ardent critic of American intervention in Vietnam, which he saw as 'delusional' because both the US and the Soviet Union had comparable strategic interests in South East Asia. And nearly four decades later, Walt and Mearsheimer (2003) challenged the extended view that Saddam Hussein posed a threat to American interests and that a military intervention was therefore unavoidable; in their opinion, Iraq was 'an unnecessary war'.

Since the 1990s, liberal interventionism has taken hold within a big part of the global human rights community. Liberal interventionists pushed the agenda of the use of force to pursue humanitarian goals like democracy promotion. Liberal interventionists were also behind the idea of the 'Responsibility to Protect' (R2P), initially formulated by an independent group of experts gathered in Canada (ICISS 2001), and partly embraced later in the UN World Summit Outcome of 2005 (UN General Assembly 2005, A/RES/60/1, para. 138–9). There is no single definition of R2P, but the bottom line is that humanity as a whole has a shared responsibility to protect civilians, militarily if need be, in case of serious human rights violations, like genocide, war crimes and crimes against humanity. For some R2P-promoters, this global responsibility would outplay other legal obligations, including the procedural requirements of Chapter VII of the UN Charter, which regulates when and how the UN Security Council can decide on the deployment of armed forces to restore international peace and security. This means that governments should feel legitimised to send their troops to countries where serious human rights abuses are taking place, even without a clear mandate from the Security Council. Although this possibility was envisioned by the ICISS, the UN General Assembly made clear in the World Summit Outcome Document that R2P could not bypass the UN Charter.

With the Rwandan genocide of 1994 still in mind, a number of observers felt compelled to justify NATO's intervention in Kosovo in 1999, despite the Security Council's failure to authorise it due to the Russian veto. For some, Kosovo would be one case only. For others, however, it would pave the way to other interventions. For example, Michael Ignatieff (2003), who had been part of the group of experts that came up with the idea of R2P, publicly defended US and British intervention in Iraq on humanitarian grounds. The R2P would later be explicitly mentioned in UN Security Council Resolution 1973 (2011) that authorised NATO's operation in Libya, which ended up in regime change. Considering the persistent instability in the country and in the region, President Obama would later regret the American decision in relation to Libya (Goldberg 2016), which pushed him not to intervene against President al-Assad in Syria, even though credible reports confirmed that he had used chemical weapons against defenceless civilians.

For two decades, part of the human rights community has relied excessively on the military. The lessons from Iraq and Libya do however suggest a change in course. Human rights advocates may prefer not to recommend the use of military force in the future. And with their stress on national interests, balance of power and prudence, realists may march by their side on this.

From Realism to an International Society Ruled by Order

E. H. Carr wrote his *Twenty Years' Crisis* (2001) to warn about what he saw as an excess of wishful thinking among the idealists of the inter-war period. Yet, he did not dismiss ideals and morality entirely. He only advocated framing them within a political structure defined mostly by national interests. Realism allows for a nuanced view of international law as the product of a pluralist international society. This was basically the idea put forward by Hedley Bull and the first generation of the English School of the 1960s and 70s, which Fred Halliday (1992, 438) liked to call 'English Realism'.

The English School accepted the realist premise of the logic of anarchy, but claimed that an international society can emerge out of that anarchy. Bull sees an international society 'when a group of states, conscious of certain common interests and common values, form a society in the sense that they conceive themselves to be bound by a common set of rules in their relations with one another, and share in the working of common institutions' (2002, 13). Order would be the axis of the international society. Bull defined order as 'a pattern that leads to a particular result, an arrangement of social life such that it promotes certain goals or values' (2002, 3–4). Order would be highly desirable because it is 'the condition of the realisation of other values', including justice (Bull 2002, 93). Order is not necessarily states' only goal, but it must outdo justice insofar as its maintenance is the primary goal. Other goals can be pursued as long as order is not put at risk.

One can indeed see international law as part of a certain idea of order in international society. Carl Schmitt himself defended this idea in *The Nomos of the Earth* (2006), where he contended that, at least since the 16th century, international law has derived from the progressive expansion of a Eurocentric notion of *nomos*, order, from the freedom of the seas, to the international law of armed conflict and the notion of state sovereignty and non-intervention. States may negotiate, draft and ratify international human rights treaties inasmuch as they do not breach the fundamental tenets of international order, among them the principle of national sovereignty. States may also set up independent human rights mechanisms (courts, criminal tribunals, committees, individual experts, etc.), but they would not necessarily feel obliged to share the interpretation of these bodies, which is likely to be inspired by a loose idea of global justice more so than by international order.

Not that far from classical realism, in the English School terminology, IHRL can be seen as the product of a political tension between a certain idea of international order, defended by some states, and a certain view of global justice, advocated by independent UN experts, scholars and NGOs. Both government officials and human rights advocates would use the same terminology of IHRL (the same standards, the same provisions of the same treaties, etc.), but they would mean different things in the above-mentioned dialectics for hegemonic contestation between utopia and apology of state action (Koskenniemi 2004 and 2005).

The implications are clear in relation to the two examples given previously. While some states will resist the expansion of the international human rights regime, some others are willing to promote it to the extent that the norms are sufficiently ambiguous and do not impose heavy burdens. For example, European states were willing to adopt the International Covenant on Economic, Social and Cultural Rights with its Article 2(1), which makes clear that obligations will depend on 'available resources' and rights are only to be fulfilled 'progressively'. Likewise, European states endorse the R2P programmatically, provided it is made compatible with the procedures of the UN Charter, and knowing that they would not have to suffer the consequences of a foreign intervention on their soil. While scholars and practitioners in general are moved by a sense of justice, solidarity and a genuine concern for the well-being of others, the hedged realism of the English School recommends them not to disregard the fact that governments are motivated by different factors linked to order.

Conclusion

This paper has advocated a measured change for human rights defenders and academics to open up to what realism has to offer. For the most part, realism and human rights have at the very least ignored each other. This paper, however, has shown three ways in which human rights could do better with a pinch of realism. Realism invites us to reflect on the political reasons why some claims are more salient than others in IHRL. Realism advises prudence in the use of military force. And adjacent to realism, we can conceptualise IHRL as the product of a political tension between order and justice in international society.

I do not intend to twist realism to make it say what most realists would not feel comfortable with. This paper is not denying that realists are sceptical of normative values in global politics. Regardless of their personal beliefs and preferences, as academics, realists would only care about the human rights situation in other countries if that situation may result in regional instability or a shift in the balance of power. I also believe realists have a hard time explaining why states agree to the creation of independent human rights bodies they have no control over, as weak as these bodies are. I cannot imagine how they could explain the high degree of state compliance with the judgments of the European Court of Human Rights. More generally, realists cannot account for the existence of an international regime that imposes non-reciprocal obligations on states. States' human rights obligations are not borne towards each other, but towards their own people, or, even more, towards anybody within their jurisdiction.

Realism is not well placed to explain the international human rights regime, and at least in their role of interpreters of global politics, realists will not become human rights activists unless they stop being realist first.

However, this paper has argued that there are areas of potential strategic interaction between human rights and realism. As noted by Rosenberg (1990, 299), realists grow stronger when criticised on ethical grounds, because such criticism gives realism the opportunity to proclaim its alleged value-free condition. Let us not criticise realism for not doing what it never intended to do. As human rights scholars and practitioners, we should instead focus on engaging with realism if only to get a better sense of the different understandings of the world we intend to change. Paraphrasing Cox, 'to change the world, we have to begin with an understanding of the world as it is, which means the structures of reality that surround us' (1986, 242). Simply ignoring the reality one seeks to transform is a guarantee of failure.

References

Agamben, Giorgio. 2005. *State of Exception*. Chicago: University of Chicago Press.

Bull, Hedley. 2002. *The Anarchical Society: A Study of Order in World Politics*. London: Palgrave.

Carr, E. H. 2001. *The Twenty Years' Crisis*. London: Palgrave MacMillan.

Cox, Robert. 1986. "Social Forces, States and World Orders: Beyond International Relations Theory". *Neorealism and Its Critics*, edited by Robert Keohane. 204–254. New York: Columbia University Press.

Donnelly, Jack. 2008. "The Ethics of Realism". *The Oxford Handbook of International Relations*, edited by Christian Reus-Smit and Duncan Snidal. Oxford: Oxford University Press, 150–162.

Freeman, Michael. 2002. *Human Rights: An interdisciplinary approach*. Cambridge: Polity.

Goldberg, Jeffrey. 2016. "The Obama Doctrine". *The Atlantic* 317(3): 70–90.

Goldsmith, Jack, and Posner, Eric. 2005. *The Limits of International Law*. Oxford: Oxford University Press.

Halliday, Fred. 1992. "International Society As Homogeneity: Burke, Marx, Fukuyama". *Millennium – Journal of International Studies* 21(3): 435–461.

Ignatieff, Michael. 2003. "Why Are We In Iraq?; (And Liberia? And Afghanistan?)". *The New York Times*, 7 September (http://www.nytimes.com/2003/09/07/magazine/why-are-we-in-iraq-and-liberia-and-afghanistan.html accessed 31/05/2017)

International Commission on Intervention and State Sovereignty (ICISS). 2001. *The Responsibility to Protect*. Ottawa: International Development Research Centre.

Kennan, George. 1985. "Morality and Foreign Policy". *Foreign Affairs* 64(2): 205–218.

Koskenniemi, Martti. 1999. "The Effects of Rights on Political Culture". *The EU and Human Rights*, edited by Philip Alston, 99–116. Oxford: Oxford University Press.

Koskenniemi, Martti. 2004. "International law and hegemony: a reconfiguration". *Cambridge Review of International Affairs* 17(2): 197–218.

Koskenniemi, Martti. 2005. *From Apology to Utopia: The Structure of International Legal Argument*. Cambridge: Cambridge University Press.

Krasner, Stephen. 1993. "Sovereignty, Regimes, and Human Rights". *Regime Theory and International Relations*, edited by Volker Rittberger. Oxford: Oxford University Press, 139–167.

Krasner, Stephen. 2002. "Realist Views of International Law". *Proceedings of the Annual Meeting (American Society of International Law)* 96: 265–8.

Landman, Todd. 2006. *Studying Human Rights*. Oxon: Routledge.

Lettinga, Doutje, and van Troost, Lars (eds.). 2015. *Can human rights bring social justice? Twelve essays*. Amsterdam: Amnesty International Netherlands.

Mahanty, Daniel. 2013. "Realists, Too, Can Stand for Human Rights". *The National Interest*, October.

Mearsheimer, John. 1994/95. "The False Promise of International Institutions". *International Security* 19(3): 5–49.

Mearsheimer, John. 1995. "A Realist Reply". *International Security* 20(1): 82–93.

Mearsheimer, John. 2014. "America Unhinged". *The National Interest*, January (available on http://nationalinterest.org/article/america-unhinged-9639, accessed 31/05/2017).

Mearsheimer, John and Walt, Stephen. 2003. "An unnecessary war". *Foreign Policy*, January (http://foreignpolicy.com/2009/11/03/an-unnecessary-war-2/, accessed 31/05/2017)

Morgenthau, Hans. 1940. "Positivism, Functionalism, and International Law". *The American Journal of International Law* 34(2): 260–284.

Morgenthau, Hans. 1948. "The Twilight of International Morality". *Ethics* 58(2): 79–99.

Morgenthau, Hans. 1965. "We Are Deluding Ourselves in Vietnam". *The New York Times*, 18 April.

Morgenthau, Hans. 1979. *Human Rights and Foreign Policy*. New York: Council on Religion and International Affairs.

Posner, Eric. 2014. *The Twilight of Human Rights Law*. Oxford: Oxford University Press.

Rosenberg, Justin. 1990. "What's the Matter with Realism?". *Review of International Studies* 16(4): 285–303.

Schmitt, Carl. 2006. *The Nomos of the Earth: In the International Law of the Jus Publicum Europeaum*. New York: Telos Press.

Schmitt, Carl. 2007. *The Concept of the Political*. Chicago: The University of Chicago Press.

Schulz, William. 2001. *In Our Own Best Interest: How Defending Human Rights Benefits Us All*. Boston: Beacon Press.

Stammers, Neil. 2009. *Human Rights and Social Movements*. London: Pluto Press.

United Nations General Assembly. 2005. *Resolution 60/1. World Summit Outcome*, 24 October, UN doc: A/RES/60/1.

Walt, Stephen. 2016. "Why Is American So Bad at Promoting Democracy in Other Countries?". *Foreign Policy*, April (http://foreignpolicy.com/2016/04/25/why-is-america-so-bad-at-promoting-democracy-in-other-countries/, accessed 31/05/2017).

12

Why IR Realism Persists

M.J. PETERSON

In a world of International Relations theory dominated by discussions of globalisation, interconnection, capitalism, ecological crisis, norms, beliefs, global civil society, and world culture, realism seems irrelevant. This is not surprising given its roots in the very different 18th century world of lightly connected and sharply competitive dynastic states. Even in analysing conflict, its lessons, drawn largely from studying inter-state wars, seem less relevant to an era dominated by internal wars than does understanding the psychological and social-psychological roots of the ethnic hatreds, religious intolerance, and other human impulses that fuel so much internal strife. Yet, in certain fundamentals, the world has not changed as much as many contemporary IR theorists believe, and realist thought remains relevant. This chapter will identify the extent of that relevance in three steps. It begins by outlining the three knowledge domains that need to be mastered to develop an adequate understanding of international relations, then indicates how realist approaches fall well short of providing understanding in two of them, followed by indicating why realist approaches remain central to understanding in the third. The conclusion affirms that, while realism alone is insufficient for understanding international relations, its insights remain necessary to that enterprise.

For all the talk of transformation, international relations remain a multi-level phenomenon. These levels have been defined in various ways. One is by geographic size, as a global system, within which exist territorial states, within which in turn exist sub-state units. Some define the levels horizontally, as a mutual interaction between a globe-spanning 'world of states' led by governments concerned with their domestic constituencies and an equally globe-spanning 'world of humans' interacting as individuals and through their own organisations across state borders. A third way, most clearly reflected in Kenneth Waltz's *Man, the State, and War* (1959) identifies humans, states (more accurately, governments as managers of political communities living in territorial states), and the international system (the politically decentralised world context in which the territorial states co-exist), as the distinct levels. Contemporary states remain territorial entities encompassing more or less well-integrated communities of humans, with governments capable of mustering more resources and coordinated activity than any non-state actors. Thus, Waltz's conception of human, state, and international system as distinct levels remains a powerful intellectual framework for sorting out causal patterns in international relations.

Realism has four main weaknesses. Three of these weaknesses, which inspire much of the criticism against realism, appear at what Waltz identifies as the human and state levels of analysis. First, realism has typically relied on a gloomy view of humans derived from assuming a supposedly unchanging conflict-prone 'human nature.' This leads to the second weakness, a tendency to treat politics both within and between states as involving unending competition for advantage. Third, realists lack clearly articulated theories of how governments of states (or any other type of actor) make decisions. The fourth weakness spans the state and international system levels, and consists of insufficient attention to the increased influence of non-state actors resulting from changes at both of those levels in the last 150 or so years. Conversely, realism's continued strengths derive from the attention realists pay to the structure and the process at the international system level. The shape of that system level does not directly determine the choices of governments and other actors, but it does constrain their choices significantly and shape the outcomes of their interactions. Each of the next three sections focuses on one of Waltz's levels of analysis, outlining how realists address each and indicating the weaknesses and strengths of realist approaches to phenomena at that level.

Humans

Realists' concerns with humans, and particularly 'human nature' as a starting point for theorising, is well-expressed in Hans Morgenthau's claim that 'politics, like society in general, is governed by objective laws that have their roots in human nature,' a human nature 'that has not changed since the classical philosophies of China, India, and Greece endeavoured to discover those laws' (1954, 3). Yet, in recent decades the notions that there is a clear divide between the 'objective' and the 'subjective' and that there is a singular human nature have been subjected to withering attack in philosophical, philosophy of science, psychological, feminist, and anthropological literatures.

Contemporary realists, like most IR theorists, avoid deep engagement in contemporary philosophical debates about the subjective and objective.

Contemporary realists are also much less likely to invoke generalised notions of 'human nature' in their arguments, though can identify enough greed, aggressiveness, cheating, and other forms of bad behaviour in both inter-individual and inter-group activity to maintain their view of politics as highly conflictual. They can sidestep debates about whether there is some overall 'human nature' and what it might be by focusing on results of recent work in human cognition to emphasise how processes of perception and misperception affect governments' choices and themselves encourage conflict (e.g., Jervis 1976, Wohlforth 1993). Thus, contemporary realists have backed away from some of the very strong assumptions about human cognition and conduct prevalent in earlier decades without discarding their overall expectation that interactions among states are likely to be competitive and conflictual.

Government Decision-Making

Realists' low level of interest in the details of decision-making is not surprising. They generally regard explaining decisions and choices as less important than understanding the implications for states and other actors operating within global decentralisation and a thin set of shared norms for interaction. In their view, the competitive pressures that exist in a decentralised system also characterised by few sources of normative restraint on conduct significantly constrain the alternatives available to any government concerned, as it should be, with its state's security and persistence over time. This stance is not surprising in light of the history of realism's long gestation. Insights that we now regard as elements of the realist theory had emerged well before the interwar period, so were available even before E. H. Carr (1939) launched his withering critique of what he regarded as the overly idealistic approach to international relations prevailing in the 1920s. Realists' focus on action within a highly competitive states system mirrored the concerns of rulers, ministers of state, and diplomats after the Peace of Westphalia (1648) established the basic outlines of the European system of territorial states. Notions of effective policy and negotiation techniques were expressed in the 17th and 18th century 'manuals for princes' (e.g. Callières 1716) and modes of coexistence through the acceptance of common rules of conduct outlined in the early writings on 'the law of nations' (Grotius 1625, Pufendorf 1672, Vattel 1758). Since most governments were not directly accountable to the populations of their state and there was only a modest level of cross-border interaction, governments were able to maintain a fairly clear separation between 'domestic politics' and 'foreign policy' or 'diplomacy.'

Conditions changed later. The late 18th and early 19th centuries were marked by the rise of democracy and nationalism. The mid and late 19th century were a period of increasing cross-border interactions in trade, finance, travel, science, and culture, and greater ideological divergence as the international workers movement posed strong challenges to established ways. The 1930s were dominated by an intense three-sided ideological contention culminating in total war among democratic, fascist, and Leninist blocs. All these developments meant that the neat separation between 'domestic politics' and 'foreign policy' prevailing in the mid-18th century progressively weakened and even the governments of great powers were no longer as uniformly insulated from domestic or transnational influences as they had been.

Under these new circumstances, realist theory's lack of explanations for government decision-making increasingly appeared to be a serious weakness. IR theorists reacted in one of two ways. Some sought to expand the realist tradition by combining realist insights about the international system with particular theories of how governments perceive, choose, and act. Kenneth Waltz provided a rallying point for one such effort, using a rational choice conception of government decision-making in *Theory of International Politics* (1979). Later efforts along these lines have reflected the modifications of rational choice theory propounded in earlier years but also rest on making strong assumptions about governments as egoistic rational utility maximisers able, in the final analysis, to act in a coherent way for their state (e.g., Fearon 1995, Grieco 1996). Other realists, most notably Robert Gilpin (1981, 2001), acknowledge linkages between the international and domestic levels in their more theoretically eclectic approach to understanding state behaviour. Some IR theorists outside the realist camp went further, filling the gap by locating the primary influences on foreign policy within the domestic level. This was most prominently expressed in the democratic peace hypothesis (e.g. Doyle 1997, Lipson 2003) placing domestic regime-types at the centre of explanations regarding foreign policy decisions and outcomes in the international system. Yet domestic-centred explanations are also prominent in examinations of international trade (e.g. Mansfield and Milner 2012).

Not all IR theorists are satisfied by either the Waltzian ignoring of domestic factors nor the claims that the primary causes of state behaviour exist at the domestic level. IR theorists inspired by historical sociology have focused analysis on the country-specific processes by which governments address the dual challenge of maintaining themselves domestically through a strong state-society connection and adjusting to challenges emanating from changing external political and economic developments (e.g. Hobson 1997). Another group, taking inspiration from Antonio Gramsci, understands international and state levels as linked by contentions over governing ideas shaping politics at both levels (e.g. van Apeldoorn 2002, Gill 2003). Rationalist theorists (e.g.

Putnam 1988) have conceptualised inter-state negotiations as a two-level game: an interaction in which chiefs of governments are simultaneously trying to negotiate agreements with each other while also paying attention to what sorts of agreements will win sufficient support at home among attentive publics and other mobilised groups to be carried out.

Intensified interconnection between states has inspired another line of criticism, one rejecting realists' continued emphasis on politico-military (or 'security') concerns as the primary focus of foreign policy. Realists never denied the relevance of other sorts of concerns; they simply maintained the older conception, widely shared among 19th century rulers and diplomats, that the 'high politics' of security and politico-military competition was not strongly affected by the 'low politics' of trade, investment, and other activities of private individuals or entities. This separation of political and all other concerns, and the consequent tendency to focus primarily on governments' interactions with other governments, gave Realism what another group of critics regard as an overly 'state-centric' view of international relations. These critics sometimes challenge the adequacy of state-centric conceptions for understanding even the 19th century, pointing to governments' susceptibility to influences exerted by what today are called transnational advocacy movements – most notably the anti-slavery movement (Iriye 2002) or trans-governmental networks of officials or experts – such as the bureaucratic reformers behind the development of intergovernmental organisations for technical and administrative cooperation in the 19th century (Murphy 1994).

Similar criticisms stem from a long tradition of highlighting the impact of economic issues and economically-motivated actors. The latter can be the transnational capitalist class emphasised by Marxists in their calls for organisation of an equally transnational-minded proletariat to end their domination (e.g. Marx and Engels 1848) as well as the communities of bankers and traders long viewed as exerting pressure against war (e.g. Angell 1909). Many contemporary theorists point to a broader set of transnational advocacy coalitions and social movements (e.g. Keck and Sikkink 1998, Kaldor 2004). Greater transnational ties and wider expectations about what governments should be doing in the realm of domestic politics have also combined to expand the foreign policy agenda beyond older concerns with coexistence to building cooperation in the face of shared problems like environmental degradation, cross-border crime, or controlling infectious diseases.

The current debates about how and how far domestic politics and the economic and other interconnections among societies pose serious challenges to realist theorising by increasing the salience of the politics within states and the growing interconnections among societies. Both developments allow other theorists to make persuasive claims that realism is sufficiently wrong to be irrelevant today.

International System

No one challenges the observation that the world remains politically decentralised. However, IR theorists disagree strongly on how international relations play out within that decentralised condition. Part of the debate involves how to define the most important element of the system structure. For realists, the political decentralisation is primary because it means that the problem of assuring security must be solved by individual states through self-strengthening, alliances, or policies of neutrality regarding the fights of others. Particularly in the neorealist vision propounded by Waltz (1979) this leads to a particular view of system-level processes as dominated by considerations of state power in a world where the possibility of war can never be ignored. Marxist (e.g. Jessop 1990; Rosenberg 1994), world-systems (e.g. Wallerstein 1974, Chase-Dunn and Hall 1997, summarised for newcomers in Wallerstein 2004) and dependency theorists (e.g. Amin 1976; Cardoso and Felatto 1979) all offer an alternative view of system structure, defining it as produced by the workings of a global capitalist economy. This leads to a very different view of system-level processes in which competition for economic position, not for maintaining or augmenting their state's power, provides governments' primary motivation.

For all their disagreements on particular points, Marxist, world-systems, and dependency theorists have a similar view of the international-level processes of interaction: they are defined by the dynamics of class struggle; even the world-system and dependency discussions of conflict between core and periphery states have a class dimension since political penetration of peripheral state elites by dominant classes in the core assures that – short of global revolution – the core remains in control. However, their shared assumption that political leaders and government bureaucrats serve as agents of the capitalists and have no independent interests of their own has been strongly contested by analysts emphasising the continuing importance of political and military concerns (e.g., Chirot 1986, Mann 1988, Tilly 1990).

Analysts who continue to view security and political concerns as primary have developed a wider variety of ideas about international-level processes. For realists, the political decentralisation of the world puts states into a competitive situation in which governments are impelled to focus on 'interests defined as power' (Morgenthau 1954, 5). This competitive milieu requires state leaders who want to maintain their state over the long haul to analyse their situation, choose, and behave in broadly similar ways (e.g. Mearsheimer 2001; Walt 2005). While agreeing that the international system remains decentralised, other groups of IR theorists have developed other visions of system level process that challenge the realist emphasis on an enduring logic of security-focused competition. English school theorists launched their notion of a 'society of states' to argue that certain fundamental practices of international politics guide government decisions more than typically assumed in realist thinking (e.g., Bull 1977; Wight 1977) and are maintained through processes of mutual socialisation indicating what is or is not acceptable conduct (e.g., Clark 2005). Constructivist theorists, drawing to varying degrees on linguistic and cognitive theories of meaning, argued that the system process is malleable – or, as Alexander Wendt put it, 'anarchy is what states make of it' (1992). Though disagreeing on the precise pathways through which meanings are formed, constructivists, ranging from those influenced by sociological institutionalism (e.g. Finnemore 1996) to those inspired by critical theory (e.g. Fuchs and Kratochwil 2002), all agree that there is no intrinsic reason political decentralisation is always marked by thin sets of shared norms; governments and other actors can shape those norms as they remake their view of the world. For constructivists, then, decentralisation is compatible with the operation of thicker sets of norms that provide more limits to choices and conduct than does the Realist version of unending and unremitting security competition. Feminist theorists agree on the malleability of system process, attributing much of its current highly competitive form to the predominance of masculine notions of how the world works (Tickner 2001, Shepherd 2010, Goldstein 2011).

A separate challenge to realist depictions of the system level stems from changes in the level of interconnection between states and societies. These involve not only higher levels of cross-border trade and financial flows since the mid-20th century, but also more contact between peoples and wider diffusion of ideas, images, clothing styles, cuisine, and other aspects of daily life. This challenge asserts the reality and impact of what was once called 'complex interdependence' (Keohane and Nye 1977), but is now generally called 'globalisation.' Whatever it is labelled, strong interconnection between members of the societies living within territorial states is viewed as creating conditions in which states have shared as well as competing interests, and governments need to modify the pattern of their interactions to address shared concerns. In the mid-1980s, a new generation of IR theorists began combining liberal and institutionalist arguments into claims that shared sets of rules for conduct in various areas and formal institutions, such as intergovernmental organisations, moderate the intensity of competition (e.g. Keohane 1984, Oye 1985; Ikenberry 2001). Increasing interconnection also inspired a world society approach maintaining that increasing interchange among societies and networks of non-state actors was creating a new set of expectations regarding governments' management of their states' external relations – not just with other states but also with societies outside their own borders (e.g. Meyer et al. 1997, Boli and Thomas 1999).

Even those IR theorists who regard state-level factors or interconnection as the primary influences on individual states' choices and actions acknowledge that the decentralised character of the international system influences outcomes by impelling states into interaction regardless of whether they seek to cooperate or to compete. Thus, even they acknowledge that understanding the international system level and the features of its structure and process remains essential to effective analysis and participate in as well as follow the continuing debate about how the international system functions and what sorts of constraints it actually creates. Both of the main system-level debates noted above – about whether political or economic considerations are the primary driver of competition and about whether interconnection is significant enough to alter the balance between competitive and cooperative drives – continue unabated. As with the debates at the human and state levels, the debate about the character of the international system proceeds partly on the basis of logic and partly on the basis of what conception seems most useful for understanding and explaining world affairs.

The Place of Realism Today

As the continuing debates among rival theoretical schools indicate, analysts of international relations have not converged on any single conception about how best to analyse, interpret, and understand international relations (see summaries of the field in, e.g., Booth and Smith 1995, Weber 2004, Burchill et al. 2005, Baylis, Smith and Owens 2008, Jackson and Sørensen 2013). Contemporary events, particularly those occurring since the end of the Cold War, have either produced – through the end of the then-prevailing bipolar balance – or opened up opportunities to more clearly perceive significant changes in the patterns of interaction among the states and other actors on the world scene.

Two changes receive the most attention. There is wide agreement that the level of interconnection prevailing before 1914 was not attained again until the 1970s, and has been exceeded today because the interconnections are not just in trade and finance. Movements of individuals and families from place to place occurred earlier, but the later 20th century provided transportation and communication technologies more conducive to maintaining contact and organising 'diasporas' to influence home country developments or cross-border relations. The intensifications of economic connections through global supply chains and global marketing have inspired claims about the rise of the trading state (Rosecrance 1986), and of a global culture or polity (e.g., Meyer et al. 1997, Boli and Thomas 1999). Nor can contemporary analysts of international relations ignore the steep reduction in international war and the significant reduction in the total number of casualties inflicted in both international and internal armed conflict since 1945. This has inspired claims that war is obsolescent (Mueller 1989, Goldstein 2001) and that this obsolescence strongly influences the conduct of territorial states. The strength of these developments explain why, as William Wohlforth (2011) noted, most IR theorists now regard realism with its emphasis on war in a state-centric world as outdated and irrelevant.

Yet, as the current example of Syria reminds us, there is nothing inevitable about the post-1945 developments. The reduction in warfare and war-caused human suffering is notable, and the literature on security communities (e.g., Adler and Barnett 1998,) suggests that there are ways states can remove resorting to armed force from their foreign-policy repertoires vis-a-vis one another. However, what Deutsch (1957) called 'non-amalgamated security communities' – groups of non-fighting states in which the participating states remain independent – take a long time to build and do not expand easily beyond regional borders. Economic and social interconnection do matter, but it remains unclear whether interconnections would now prove to be a bulwark against a world war or would be broken up as easily as they were in 1914 and after the Great Depression. Feminist arguments about the strong differences between 'male' and 'female' ways of thinking have also been challenged by arguments that many of the gender differences presented as 'hardwired' are more the products of social expectations than of intrinsic working of human brains (e.g., Fine 2011). Optimism about the spread of democracy has been replaced by worry about revivals of xenophobic forms of nationalism in many parts of the world.

All of the changes in phenomena or in human understanding of them at each level of analysis have not altered the fact that international relations remain multi-level. Good explaining and understanding require taking all levels into account. Realism has not developed good tools for understanding the human and state levels; at those levels analytical tools generated by other traditions of theorising must be brought to bear. Though 20th and 21st century developments suggest that the system level is not equivalent to Thomas Hobbes's (1651) conception of life in the 'state of nature,' the default mode of international conduct – the one chosen when no other considerations or conditions incline actors toward doing otherwise – remains much more opportunistic and self-help oriented than the default mode of conduct within reasonably well-ordered territorial states. As a strong tradition within rational choice theory explains, the tone of interaction in society as a whole depends on the relative prevalence of 'co-operators' willing to temper immediate self-advancement for longer-term shared gain, and 'non-co-operators' always seeking their individual immediate advantage. Normative restraints are stronger when co-operators predominate, but even when they do predominate, co-operators need to adopt strategies for interaction that will limit the gains accruing to non-co-operators so that normative restraints will be maintained and cooperation remains the best choice (e.g. Axelrod 1997; Doebeli, Hauert and Killingback 2004, Nowak 2006). The continuing problem of dealing with non-co-operators means that the realist warnings that governments of states need to keep a wary eye on other actors and be ready to defend themselves and their own states remain relevant.

In sum, the causal mechanisms leading to actor perceptions, choices, and behaviours and the conjunctions of factors shaping the outcomes of their interactions are too complex to be understood using only realist theory. However the world remains decentralised and sufficiently competitive that the realist analyses of power politics and of how differences in material and organisational capability are brought to bear in interacting and using capability advantages to gain more influence over outcomes remain essential to understanding choices, actions and outcomes. IR Realism is not sufficient for understanding and explaining international politics, but its concerns with power politics in a decentralised system remain necessary. That is why it persists.

*Author note: Thanks to Vinnie Ferraro, Jane Fountain, Peter Haas, Ray LaRaja, Paul Musgrave and Kevin Young for helpful conversations, and to J. R. Avgustin and Max Nurnus for encouragement and comments on earlier drafts.

References

Adler, Emanuel and Michael Barnett. 1998. *Security Communities*. Cambridge: Cambridge University Press.

Angell, Norman. 1909. *The Great Illusion: A Study of the Relation of Military Power to National Advantage*. London: William Heinemann.

Amin, Samir. 1976. *Unequal Development: An Essay on the Social Formations of Peripheral Capitalism*. New York: Monthly Review Press.

Apeldoorn, Bastiaan van. 2002. *Transnational Capitalism and the Struggle over European Integration*. London: Routledge.

Axelrod, Robert. 1997. *The Evolution of Complexity: Agent-Based Models of Cooperation and Competition*. Princeton, NJ: Princeton University Press.

Baylis, John, Steve Smith, and Patricia Owens, eds. 2008. *The Globalisation of World Politics.* 4th edition. Oxford: Oxford University Press.

Boli, John and George M. Thomas, eds. 1999. *Constructing World Culture: International Nongovernmental Organizations since 1875*. Stanford, CA: Stanford University Press.

Booth, Ken and Steve Smith, eds. 1995. *International Relations Theory Today*. Cambridge: Polity Press.

Bull, Hedley. 1977. *The Anarchical Society*. London: Macmillan and New York: Columbia University Press.

Burchill, Scott, Andrew Linklater, Richard Devetek, Jack Donnelly, Terry Nardin, Matthew Patterson, Christian Reus-Smit and Jacqui True. 2005. *Theories of International Relations*. London: Palgrave.

Cardoso, Fernando Henrique and Enzo Felatto. 1979. *Dependency and Development in Latin America*. Berkeley: University of California Press.

Chase-Dunn, Christopher K., and Thomas D. Hall. 1997. *Rise and Demise: Comparing World – Systems.* Boulder, CO: Westview Press.

Callières, François de. 1716. *De la manière de négocier avec les souverains* (On the Manner of Negotiating with Princes; sometimes titled On Diplomacy).

Carr, E.H. 1939. *The Twenty Years' Crisis 1919–1939*. London: Macmillan.

Chirot, Daniel. 1986. *Social Change in the Modern Era.* San Diego: Harcourt Brace Jovanovich.

Clark, Ian. 2005. *Legitimacy in International Relations.* Oxford: Oxford University Press.

Deutsch, Karl. 1957. *Political Community and the North American Area.* Princeton: Princeton University Press.

Doebeli, Michael, Christoph Hauert, and Timothy Killingback. 2004. "The Evolutionary Origin of Co-operators and Defectors". *Science* 306 (5697): 859–862.

Doyle, Michael W. 1997. *Ways of War and Peace*. New York: W.W. Norton.

Fearon, James D. 1995. "Rationalist Explanations for War". *International Organization*, 49(3): 379–414.

Fine, Cordelia. 2011. *Delusions of Gender: How Our Minds, Society, and Neurosexism Create Difference*. New York: W.W. Norton.

Finnemore, Martha. 1996. *National Interests in International Society.* Ithaca, NY: Cornell University Press.

Fuchs, Doris and Friedrich Kratochwil, eds. 2002. *Transformative Change and Global Order.* Berlin: LIT Verlag.

Gill, Stephen. 2003. *Power and Resistance in the New World Order*. London: Palgrave.

Gilpin, Robert. 1981. *War and Change in World Politics*. Princeton, NJ: Princeton University Press.

Gilpin, Robert. 2001. *Global Political Economy: Understanding the International Economic Order*. Princeton, NJ: Princeton University Press.

Goldstein, Joshua. 2001. *War and Gender: How Gender shapes the War System and Vice-Versa.* Cambridge: Cambridge University Press.

Goldstein, Joshua. 2011. *Winning the War on War: The Decline of Armed Conflict Worldwide* New York: Dutton Penguin.

Grieco, Joseph. 1996. "State Interests and International Rule Trajectories: A Neorealist Interpretation of the Maastricht Treaty and European Economic and Monetary Union". *Security Studies* 5: 176–222.

Grotius, Hugo. 1625. *De Jure Belli ac Pacis* (On the Law of War and Peace).

Hobbes, Thomas. 1651. *Leviathan*.

Hobson, John M. 1997. *The Wealth of States: A Comparative Sociology of International Economic and Political Change*. Cambridge: Cambridge University Press.

Ikenberry, John G. 2001. *After Victory: Institutions, Strategic Restraint and the Rebuilding of Order after Major Wars*. Princeton, NJ: Princeton University Press.

Iriye, Akira. 2002. *Global Community: The Role of International Organizations in the Making of the Contemporary World*. Berkeley: University of California Press.

Jackson, Robert H. and Georg Sørensen. 2013. *Introduction to International Relations: Theories and Approaches*. 5th edition. Oxford: Oxford University Press.

Jervis, Robert. 1976. *Perception and Misperception in World Politics*. Princeton, NJ: Princeton University Press.

Jessop, Bob. 1990. *State Theory*. Cambridge: Polity Press.

Kaldor, Mary. 2004. *Global Civil Society: An Answer to War*. Cambridge: Polity Press.

Keck, Margaret and Kathryn Sikkink. 1998. *Activists beyond Borders: Advocacy Networks in International Politics*. Ithaca, NY: Cornell University Press.

Keohane, Robert O. 1984. *After Hegemony*. Princeton, NJ: Princeton University Press.

Keohane, Robert O. and Joseph S. Nye, Jr. 1977. *Power and Interdependence*. Boston: Little, Brown.

Lipson, Charles. 2003. *Reliable Partners: How Democracies Have Made a Separate Peace*. Princeton University Press.

Mann, Michael. 1988. *States, War, and Capitalism*. Oxford: Basil Blackwell.

Mansfield, Edward D. and Helen V Milner. 2012. *Votes, Vetos, and the Political Economy of International Trade Agreements*. Princeton, NJ: Princeton University Press.

Marx, Karl and Friedrich Engels. 1848. *The Communist Manifesto*.

Mearsheimer, John J. 2001. *The Tragedy of Great Power Politics*. New York: W.W. Norton.

Meyer, John W., John Boli, George M. Thomas, and Francisco O. Ramirez. 1997. "World Society and the Nation-State". *American Journal of Sociology* 103(1): 144–181.

Morgenthau, Hans. 1954. *Politics among Nations*. 2nd edition. New York: Alfred A. Knopf.

Mueller, John. 1989. *Retreat from Doomsday: The Obsolescence of Major War*. New York: Basic Books.

Murphy, Craig. 1994. *International Organization and Industrial Change*. Cambridge: Polity Press.

Nowak, Martin A. 2006. "Five Rules for the Evolution of Cooperation". *Science* 314(5805): 1560–3.

Oye, Kenneth, ed. 1985. *Cooperation under Anarchy. International Organization*, 38(1).

Pufendorf, Samuel von. 1672. *De iure naturae et gentium* (On the Law of Nature and of Nations).

Putnam, Robert. 1988. "Diplomacy and Domestic Politics: The Logic of Two-Level Games". *International Organization*, 41(3): 427–460.

Rosecrance, Richard. 1986. *The Rise of the Trading State: Commerce and Conquest in the Modern World*. New York: Basic Books.

Rosenberg, Justin. 1994. *The Empire of Civil Society*. London: Verso.

Shepherd, Laura J, ed. 2010. *Gender Matters in Global Politics: A Feminist Introduction to International Relations.* New York and London: Routledge.

Tickner, J. Ann. 2001. *Gendering World Politics: Issues and Approaches in the Post-Cold War Era.* New York, Columbia University Press.

Tilly, Charles. 1990. *Coercion, Capital, and European States.* Cambridge, MA: Basil Blackwell.

Vattel, Emerich de. 1758. *Le Droit des gens; ou, Principes de la loi naturelle appliqués à la conduite et aux affaires des nations et des souverains* (The Law of Nations; or, Principles of the Law of Nature, Applied to the Conduct and Affairs of Nations and Sovereigns).

Wallerstein, Immanuel. 1974. *The Modern World-System, vol. I: Capitalist Agriculture and the Origins of the European World-Economy in the Sixteenth Century.* New York: Academic Press.

Wallerstein, Immanuel. 2004. *World-Systems Analysis: An Introduction.* Durham, NC: Duke University Press.

Walt, Stephen. 2005. *Taming American Power: The Global Response to U.S. Primacy.* New York: W.W. Norton.

Waltz, Kenneth. 1959. *Man, The State, and War: A Theoretical Analysis.* New York: Columbia University Press.

Waltz, Kenneth. 1979. *Theory of International Politics.* New York: Random House.

Weber, Cynthia. 2004. *International Relations Theory. A Critical Introduction*, 2nd edition. London: Taylor & Francis.

Wendt, Alexander. 1992. "Anarchy is what States make of it". *International Organization* 46(2): 391–425.

Wight, Martin. 1977. *Systems of States.* Edited by Hedley Bull. Leicester: University of Leicester Press for the London School of Economics.

Wohlforth, William. 1993. *The Elusive Balance: Power and Perceptions during the Cold War.* Ithaca, NY: Cornell University Press.

Wohlforth, William. 2011. "No One Loves a Realist Explanation: The Cold War's End Revisited". *International Politics,* 8(4/5): 441–459.

Note on Indexing

E-IR's publications do not feature indexes. If you are reading this book in paperback and want to find a particular word or phrase you can do so by downloading a free PDF version of this book from the E-IR website.

View the e-book in any standard PDF reader such as Adobe Acrobat Reader (pc) or Preview (mac) and enter your search terms in the search box. You can then navigate through the search results and find what you are looking for. In practice, this method can prove much more targeted and effective than consulting an index.

If you are using apps (or devices) such as iBooks or Kindle to read our e-books, you should also find word search functionality in those.

You can find all of our e-books at: http://www.e-ir.info/publications